This book is dedicated to the men and women served in 605 and to the memory of the brave who so tragically lost their lives.

"605"
No.605 (County of Warwick) Squadron
Royal Auxiliary Air Force

Written and published by Ian Piper
Honorary Historian and Life Vice-President
605 Squadron Association

First published in 2003
ISBN No 0 9529516 1 4
605 Squadron Website: www.605squadron.com

Printed by Louis Drapkin Ltd, Birmingham; 0121 766 6663

HISTORY OF 605 SQUADRON

(Some of the following text has been taken from a scrapbook kept by the Squadron that was reformed in 1942.)

A. 1926 to the Outbreak of the War.

The Squadron was formed at Castle Bromwich in October 1926, and was one of the first group of five auxiliary Squadrons to be formed. It was a Bomber Squadron equipped with D.H. 9A's being successively re-equipped with Wapitis, Harts and Hinds. During these twelve years as a Bomber Squadron it succeeded in winning the Esher Trophy (an inter-auxiliary squadron efficiency test) in 1927, 1930, 1931, 1933, 1934 and 1935. On the 1st January 1939 they were concerted to a Fighter Squadron, and transferred to No.11. Fighter Group. In May 1939 the squadron was re-equipped with Gladiators, and when war broke out was in the process of re-equipping with Hurricanes.

Up to the outbreak of war the squadron was run on a complete auxiliary basis. The auxiliary Officers and airmen, who were for the most part fully occupied in their various civil vocations in the County of Warwick, devoted all their week-ends and any spare evenings they could in mid week to attending at the Station, and learning their job under the Regular personnel consisting of an Adjutant, Asst/Adjt and Equipment officer, and from 60 to 70 N.C.O's and airmen who acted as instructors.

1935: A formation of 605 Squadron Hawker Hinds

It may not always be realised that the average pilot of those days, with his keenness and enthusiasm, was able to put in more flying hours in the year than many officers in regular squadrons. In June 1936 the squadron completed 380 hours flying, which was at that time considered a very high figure for any squadron.

The squadron was selected to participate in the annual Royal Review of the Royal Air Force at Mildenhall held in connection with the Jubilee Celebrations of His Majesty, King George V. The Squadron has on several occasions taken part in the Air Exercises in connection with Air Defence of Great Britain. On one occasion the Squadron had the honour of receiving the Trophy from H.R.H. The Prince of Wales (now Duke of Windsor). The Right honourable Viscount Bearsted M.C. became Hon. Air Commodore of the Squadron in December 1930, and was succeeded in 1938 by Sir Lindsay Everard M.P.

The Squadron was formed by S/Ldr J.A.C. Wright A.F.C. T.D., who commanded it until March 1936 when he was succeeded by S/Ldr Lord Willoughby de Broke. M.C. A.F.C.

B. Beginning of the War to after Dunkirk May 1940.

TANGMERE

At the outbreak of war the Squadron was mobilised and moved to its war Station at Tangmere, where for sometime it enjoyed the curious distinction of having one Gladiator Flight and one Hurricane Flight. The complete re-equipping with Hurricanes not being achieved until November 1939. During the Squadrons tour of duty at Tangmere, life was very quiet from an operational point of view, although much hard work was put in Day and Night, in training on Hurricanes, and by the end of the year they were fully operational with these Aircraft. They had no opportunity of engaging the enemy. They were sent up on numerous interception patrols, which generally turned out to be Air Liners or communication aircraft returning from France. Enemy aircraft crossing the sector was negligible.

In December 1939 S/Ldr Lord Willoughby de Broke handed over command of the Squadron to S/Ldr G.V. Perry.

WICK.

Early in 1940 the Squadron moved to Wick, which was then the busiest Sector in Fighter Command from an operational point of view, owing to the continued enemy attacks on Scapa Flow. It was not until April 1940 that the Squadron got its first Hun, and during their stay at Wick they were credited with 1½ enemy aircraft destroyed.

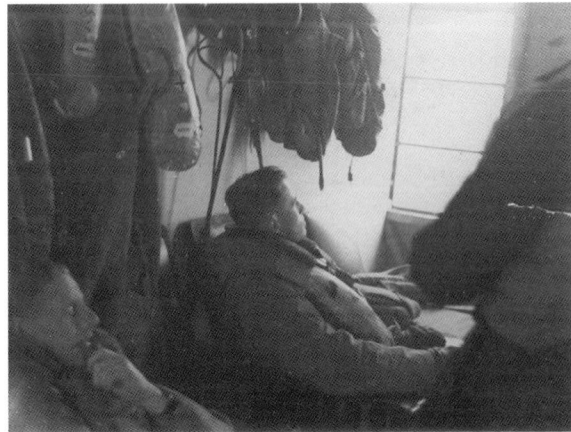

1940: 605 fighter pilots F/O Bunny Currant and F/O Graham Austin at readiness

HAWKINGE.

In the middle of May the Squadron was brought south to Hawkinge and took part in the Battle of Dunkirk. It was then substantially an auxiliary Squadron in the case of both Pilots and ground crews.

They arrived at Hawkinge with only 14 Operational Pilots, as others had previously been posted from the Squadron to fill up the gaps in the badly knocked about squadrons in France. There were hectic days, the Squadron remaining at Hawkinge for only 10 days, during which time they were reduced to eight operational pilots after it had made its last ill-fated sortie during which three pilots were lost including the Commanding Officer S/Ldr Perry.

During this time however they succeeded in destroying eleven enemy aircraft.

In their stay at Hawkinge they rarely met not less than formations of 40 enemy aircraft and operated 3 or 4 times a day from dawn to dusk, generally by themselves, but occasionally with part of another Squadron. The work of the ground crews at this time was magnificent.

C. Interim – June, July and August 1940. 13 Group.

At the end of May the squadron was withdrawn from the line and went to Drem to refit and re-equip under the command of S/Ldr W.M. Churchill. During the three months that they were there ceaseless training took place by day and by night under the untiring and inspiring command of their new Commanding Officer who had had some time before been a member of the Squadron, but had just returned from France where he was commanding No.3 Squadron, and had been awarded the D.S.O. and D.F.C. for his work with that Squadron.

In the light of the future events it is no exaggeration to state that the whole of the success of this Squadron when they came down to fight in the Battle of Britain was due to the hard training and sound tactics taught them by S/Ldr Churchill. During this time the Squadron had lost all original auxiliary pilots by posting, and received replacements from O.T.U's, but the ground crews were largely still composed of the old auxiliaries.

D. September 1940 to April 1941 11 Group.

BATTLE OF BRITAIN.

Early in September the Squadron came down full of excitement to the South and arrived at Croydon on 6th September. Two days later they were in action, and distinguished themselves, which they continued to do until the Battle of Britain had been fought and won. The Squadron was at first commanded by S/Ldr Churchill until the end of September, S/Ldr McKellar then took over and continued the inspiring leadership in the air until the 1st November when he was killed.

During the two months September and October, formations of enemy bombers, from 50 to 100 strong, with fighter escort around them were continually encountered.

In this period the Squadron destroyed over 40 enemy aircraft, probably destroyed 15, and damaged another 40 for the loss to themselves of six pilots only. In November and early December the enemy no longer sent over large formations of bombers, but many high flying small formations of fighters.

Against this, it was more difficult to score a spectacular success, but they added seven more destroyed, three probably destroyed, and ten damaged to their score, for the loss of two pilots (including S/Ldr McKellar).

As a result of their high record and good flying tactics the Squadron was rewarded by being the first fighter squadron to be re-equipped with Hurricane Mk 2 aircraft early in December. Between the 1st November and mid December the Squadron were ably led by one of their Flight Lieutenants (now W/Cdr Currant D.S.O. D.F.C. and Bar).

In the middle of December S/Ldr Edge D.F.C., one of the oldest members of the original auxiliary Squadron, was posted to command 605 Squadron. During the winter the times were quiet and the weather was bad.

Until February they had one operational flight at Croydon and one flight at Martlesham carrying out experimental work the on the new Hurricanes. In the middle of February the whole squadron was transferred to Martlesham. From then until the end of April 1941 they were engaged in Convoy Patrols off the East Coast and destroyed three more enemy bombers for no loss.

Outstanding Performance during the Battle of Britain.

The most outstanding performances during this period were: -

1. On the famous 15th September when the Squadron destroyed nine, probably destroyed two and damaged four enemy aircraft for no loss to themselves; on the 7th October when they destroyed seven and damaged four enemy aircraft for the loss of one pilot, and on 9th September when they destroyed six and probably destroyed one enemy aircraft for the loss of one pilot.

2. When S/Ldr McKellar was leading his flight into 17 He.111's flying in three vics with sections line astern with 20 Me.110's slightly above and behind them and about 50 Me.109's further above and behind again, he ordered a Head-on attack upon the bombers. S/Ldr McKellar fired from a slight dive at about 700 yards on the leader of the first bomber vic and smoke and flames issued from its wings, he then fired on the leaders left hand machine, almost at the same time the leaders machine exploded, a wing flew off the left hand machine and the right hand machine rolled over on to its back and dived down in flames all three were destroyed. This outstanding performance was thought to have been caused by the explosion of the lead machine.

3. On the 15th September, when the Squadron were attacking 30 Do.17's protected by 70 Me.109's, the lateral control of F/O Cooper-Slipper's aircraft had been rendered useless and he could only move the control column about three inches fore and aft, as he, with his section, were making a diving beam attack on the front of the on-coming bombers. Thinking his number was up and being determined to do the greatest damage at the time that was possible, he deliberately rammed one of the bombers hitting one of the second vic amidships and tearing off one of its wings, his aircraft was thrown clear of the enemy aircraft minus its port wing and most of its engine. His aircraft fell out of control in an inverted spin and he baled out landing unhurt near Maidstone, and was back with his Squadron within two hours.

E. April 1941 to November 1941.

At the end of April the Squadron were withdrawn from the line to No.9 Group, first at Baginton and then shortly to Honiley. During this period all pilots except one, who had been with the squadron either at Croydon or at Martlesham were posted to various other duties, including (in September 1941) their C.O. S/Ldr Edge, who was posted to take command of an O.T.U. at Aden.

F. Since September 1941.

605 Squadron pilots (18 in all) left Honiley in November 1941 and proceeded to Glasgow where they embarked in H.M.S. Argus, and after about a week at sea arrived at Gibraltar, where Squadron Commanders of 605, 242, 258 were summoned aboard H.M.S. Ark Royal for a conference as to how the operation of flying our Hurricanes off the

carrier were to be done. All ground crews and administrative staff remained at Honiley and it is believed left England some time during December.

It was decided that 605 and 242 Squadrons would be the first batch to be flown off, and later the Carrier would return to Gibraltar in order to fly off personnel of 258 Squadron. The question of numbers cropped up and finally it was arranged that four pilots of 605 Squadron would remain at Gibraltar and to Malta with 258 Squadron. 16 pilots of 605 Squadron flew to Malta and remained inactive until about the latter end of December. S/Ldr Reid was in command of the Squadron at this time but he was, in January 1942, invalided home and handed the Squadron over to A/Sldr Andrews D.F.M. of 242 Squadron. For a short time 605 operated as a squadron under their new Commanding Officer, and later it was decided that the pilots of 605 and 242 would be drafted to the existing squadron on the island as reinforcements for losses.

G. Ground Personnel (Far East)

The ground personnel departed Honiley in December 1941 and journeyed North by train to Gourock, Scotland. There, they boarded the appropriately named ship, The Warwick Castle and set sail 7th Dec. 1941 to an undisclosed destination. Speculation was rife. The Japanese attack on Pearl Harbour heightened the rumours as the ship set a southerly course. After two weeks at sea they docked at Freetown, Sierra Leone. On Christmas Day 1941 they left Freetown and after a brief stay at Cape Town, South Africa they continued their journey as their course took them steadily East. 605's convoy joined with another force of vessels from Durban and they continued into the Indian Ocean.

By this time the Japanese had invaded the Malay Peninsular and were now threatening the Dutch East Indies. The convoy was split in two; 605's section heading for Batavia, Java, the other for Singapore. After mooring at Tandjeon Priok, they continued their journey to Sumatra and were stationed at Palembang airfield, where they were met with constant bombardment from the Japanese. On 14th February the Japs launched a huge offensive and dropped several hundred troops by parachute on the area occupied by 605.

Several 605 men were killed in this attack and the subsequent bombing that followed. There was understandably much confusion after the Jap attack, with many different groups of airmen scattered in and around the area of Palembang airfield. Many fought back with whatever arms they could muster. Some even managed to get back to the port of Oosthaven by train. The grave news that Singapore had fallen on 15th February 1942 to the Japanese meant that the Japs could now concentrate their efforts on securing Java and Sumatra. The future for 605 looked bleak.

The Squadron joined forces with Nos. 242 and 258 Squadrons, and despite all odds, fought on for two weeks, recording a number of successes against the Japanese Air Force.

The news that the Dutch had capitulated spelt the end for the men of 605. They were now officially Prisoners of War, and the Japanese Imperial Guard began rounding up the various groups, and so began 3 1/2 years of incarceration.

Many were sent by train to a civilian prison in Boei Glodok, 30 or 40 to a cell designed to house 12. Six months later they were transported by boat to Singapore and then via the Japanese "hell-ship" the "Dai Nichi Maru" to Shimonoseki, Japan. The appalling conditions aboard the ship contributed to the deaths of many of the men in later weeks and months. To compound matters, the men had arrived in Japan in November during a fierce snowstorm, and they were still wearing their tropical kit.

The men were split into groups, some were dispatched to the island of Ambon to build a railway; some were sent to Hokkaido, some to the mines at Nagasaki, and a large group was sent to the shipbuilding town of Habu.

The men endured 3 1/2 years at the hands of the Japanese, many losing their lives to pneumonia, malaria and other tropical diseases. There were no medical personnel or supplies in the camp and what little food they were given consisted of a small bowl of rice and a cup of hot water three times a day. Some men lost as much as six stones in body weight. Those working in the shipyard at Habu did their level best to sabotage the work they were being forced to do.

At great personal risk, they would fit the wrong parts and drop nuts and bolts into the working mechanisms of the ship.

The tide of the War in the East began to turn against the Japanese and Allied raids on the dockyard became routine. It was just a matter of time before the Japs surrendered and the men of 605 were free once more. Most of the men were sent by boat to recuperate with volunteer families in Australia, as they were far too weak to survive the long journey home by sea. The darkest chapter in the history of 605 was at an end.

H. June 1942 – Reformed.

605 was reformed on the 7th June 1942 at Ford under the command of W/Cdr P.W. Townsend D.S.O. D.F.C. and the squadron was gradually equipped with Havocs and Bostons. On the 14th July W/Cdr Townsend, with P/O Palmer navigating and Sgt. Wiseman as gunner, took off in a Havoc and successfully completed the Squadron's first operation since re-forming.

On the 7th August 1942, W/Cdr G.L. Denholm D.F.C. took over command and the and the squadron continued training and operating as night intruders against enemy bombers returning to the airfields in France, Belgium and Holland after raiding Great Britain. From the 14th to the 20th August most of the aircraft and personnel moved to Hunsdon as Ford was getting crowded in preparation for the Dieppe raid. On the 19th August two of the crews who remained at Ford took part in this raid and carried out the first sorties of the day. The 20th August found all the squadron back at Ford where they remained until the 14th March 1943, excepting the period 2nd October to the 9th October 1942 when they occupied Debden.

The period on Bostons was not marked with any great successes and it was not until the squadron converted to Mosquito's in February 1943 and the range and scope of operations was increased that the score began to mount.

The "free-lance" sorties against enemy training bases and Bomber Support operations against enemy night fighters gradually overshadowed "intruders" as enemy activity against the British Isles decreased. The most successful month in this period was September when ten enemy aircraft were destroyed.

The squadron was then at Castle Camps where it had moved on 14th March 1943 and was commanded by W/Cdr C.D. Tomalin A.F.C., who succeeded W/Cdr Denholm on the 30th April 1943.

1943: 605 "Intruders", de Havilland Mosquitos NF.II

On the 25th September 1943, W/Cdr B.R.O'B. Hoare D.S.O. D.F.C. and Bar, assumed command and on the 6th October 1943 the squadron moved to Bradwell Bay. Operating from this aerodrome on the night of the 10/11th Jan. 1944, W/Cdr Hoare destroyed a Ju.188 over enemy territory and this brought the squadron score to 100 destroyed. This success was celebrated by a party at the Dorchester Hotel, London, where many pre-war members entertained thirty of the then present members of the squadron and to mark the occasion a silver model Mosquito was presented to the Squadron by Sir Lindsay Everard, M.P. Later, a claim being stepped up and confirmed as destroyed made W/Cdr Hoare's Ju.188 the 101st.

On the 7th April 1944, the squadron moved to Manston and on the 10th of this month W/Cdr N.J. Starr D.F.C. took over command. "D" day found the squadron still there and it had the honour of destroying the first enemy aircraft after "H" Hour, and many more later. The night of the 12/13th June 1944 was chosen by the Germans to launch their "secret weapon", the pilotless aircraft, against London and the main effort of the squadron was diverted to stopping the menace. A total of 73 "Divers", as they were called, were destroyed during the hours of darkness in the next few months.

On the 20th November 1944 the squadron severed its long relationship with Fighter Command and joined No.2 Group, 2nd Tactical Air Force moving to Hartford Bridge the next day. W/Cdr R.A. Mitchell, D.F.C. and Bar, assumed command on the 20th Sept. 1944 and successfully held the squadron together happily during the few weeks non-operational work which followed the change to T.A.F. Becoming operational on Christmas Day, 1944 it operated in fair weather or foul from Hartford Bridge until the 15th March 1945 when the squadron moved to Coxyde, Belgium, where it came under the shell-fire from the Germans at Dunkirk. On the 22nd February 1945 the squadron took part in operation "Clarion" and put 19 aircraft into the air in 10 minutes as part of a great daylight sweep. We lost 4 of the 19, but luckily some of the four crews survived.

At Coxyde, 605 continued harassing Hun transport and communications in all weathers by night and suffered another tragedy when the very popular C.O., W/Cdr Mitchell failed to return on the night of the 17/18th March. On the 25th April 1945, W/Cdr A.W. Horne, D.F.C., A.F.C., took over command and on the 28th moved to Volkel, Holland, where living in tents, it saw VE and VJ days and finally, at the end of August 1945, the end of 605 — for the time being.

During April 1945 the squadron flew 282 operational sorties and operated on 24 nights out of the 30; a remarkable achievement especially as both aircrews and aircraft were available were well under establishment. During the months with No.2 Group, splendid results were obtained, though the squadron's primary target changed from enemy aircraft to enemy transport, etc. It is pleasant to record, however, that on the last night of operations, F/Lt B. Williams and his navigator, W/O S.E. Hardy destroyed an Fw.190 and damaged another enemy aircraft.

This brought the squadron score since re-forming to 97 aircraft destroyed, 9 probably destroyed and 82 damaged. 75 pilotless aircraft were also destroyed and although figures for all forms of transport cannot be given, the following figures give a good indication of the success of the squadron's work in this direction;- 19 locomotive destroyed, 306 damaged and 184 barges damaged.

Since re-forming the squadron lost 38 aircraft and crews, thought 4 of these were not due to enemy action and during this period its personnel gained the following decorations and awards;- 1 Bar to the D.S.O., 7 Bars to D.F.C's., 36 D.F.C's., 1 A.F.C., 2 M.B.E's., 3 D.F.M's., 1 B.E.M., 13 Mention in Despatches.

Now, 605 is just a number, but we, the war-time members of this grand squadron who strived under many difficulties with comrades some of whom have passed on, to keep up its reputation, trust that it will regain its Auxiliary status and hope that this scrap-book will serve as a permanent record of 605's outstanding war achievements and inspire all future members to maintain the magnificent spirit and traditions that existed during the War years among its personnel. We wish those that follow us the very best of luck and feel sure that they will find in the squadron the same esprit de corps we knew in our time.

I. Re-forming as an Auxiliary Squadron 1946

605 Squadron was officially reformed as an Auxiliary unit on 10th May 1946 at RAF Honiley in Warwickshire. The Squadron had been stationed at Honiley briefly in 1941, before being posted overseas. The Squadron was designated as a Night Fighter unit under the command of S/Ldr R.J. Walker D.S.O.

Auxiliary ground crew personnel were required to attend 12 weekends and 15 days annual camp and complete a 100 hours of training per annum, and aircrew had to put in 125 hours of flying. Honiley was virtually snowed in from Jan to Apr 1947. The Squadron's first operational aircraft, Mosquito Mk30's began arriving in Apr 1947, and 3 months later 605's role changed from that of Night Fighters to Day Fighters.

A change in personal also took place in 1947, the Squadron's first CO, A/Cdr J.A.C. Wright A.F.C. T.D. took over from A/Cdr Sir Lindsay Everard D.L. J.P. as 605's Honorary Air Commodore. In December 1947 S/Ldr R.T.C. Goodwin took over command of the Squadron from S/Ldr Walker.

1948 was a proud year for 605; the Squadron were nominated as the first Auxiliary unit to receive jet aircraft when it was re-equipped with the deHavilland Vampire F.1 fighter.

Two Harvards and two Spitfires were provided to assist the pilots with the move from Mosquito's to single-seater jets. The Vampire was powered by a Goblin engine, and had a maximum speed of 540 m.p.h. and was armed with 4 x 20mm canons.

In October 1948 Stratford-upon-Avon granted the Freedom of Entry to 605 Squadron, the Royal Warwickshire Regiment and the Warwickshire Yeomanry. Four years later in 1952 605 was granted the same honour by the City of Coventry.

In July 1949 S/Ldr J.A. Timmis took over command of the Squadron from the retiring S/Ldr R.C.T. Goodwin. In June 1951 the Vampire F.1s were replaced with the more modern FB.5 variant, which was equipped to carry 2,000lbs of bombs.

605 commemorated its Silver Jubilee in 1951 with a dinner at Honiley, attended by many of the pre-war and war-time officers.

In October 1951, S/Ldr P.M.R. Walton took over from S/Ldr J.A. Timmis who had decided to emigrate to Southern Rhodesia.

1954: A formation of 605 Vampire FB.5s

One of 605's proudest moments came in March 1954 when H.R.H. Princess Margaret presented the Squadron with its Royal Standard at Honiley.

Late in 1956 a decision was taken by the powers that be that spelt the end for the Auxiliary Air Force and on 11th March 1957, No.605 (County of Warwick) Squadron was disbanded for the last time. The skies of Warwickshire fell silent once more.

605 had proudly worn the Bear and Ragged staff of Warwickshire for thirty-one years and had fought with distinction and honour, at home and overseas.

In a testament to the esprit de corps that exists amongst 605, a Squadron Association was formed in 1957, and 46 years on, the Association is as strong as ever. It's success would not of been possible without the considerable efforts of our secretary, Geoff Greenwood who has been in the post since the Association began.

1957 may of spelt the end of an era for 605, but the spirit of our proud Squadron lives on.

Honiley 1951: 605 Silver Jubilee, 6 Commanding Officers, L-R: S/Ldr John Timmis 1949-51, S/Ldr Bob Walker D.S.O. 1946-7, A/Cdr Alan Wright A.F.C. T.D. 1926-36, G/Cpt Lord Willoughby de Broke M.C. A.F.C 1936-39, S/Ldr Ron Goodwin 1947-9 & S/Ldr Martin Walton 1951-56.

1927: 605's first formation at Castle Bromwich. The above page is taken from the Squadron's "Rumble Book" which was kept to record various "offences" committed by 605's Officers. Fines were levied for such misdemeanours as line-shoots (ie bragging, showing-off), mentions in the press, crashes etc

1926: 605 Squadron's first aircraft, a dual control deHavilland 9A E8686, pictured here at Castle Bromwich.

1926: Another of the first aircraft to join 605, Avro 504N J8686.

605's first Commanding Officer, S/Ldr John Alan Cecil Wright A.F.C., T.D. (on right, pictured here as an Air Commodore) and Les Tye, the first airman to join 605 in 1926. This photograph was taken in 1951 at the Squadron's Silver Jubilee Dinner at RAF Honiley.

1926: 605's first crest.

View of Castle Bromwich airfield, taken sometime between 1922 and 1924. The Handley Page W.8b airliner, G-EBBI was operated by Handley Page Transport.

Late 1920's: RAF Castle Bromwich, Birmingham

1929: 605 recruitment march through the centre of Birmingham

View of Castle Vale/Castle Bromwich taken by the author in 1990 from an RAF Hercules. It's interesting to compare this view to the photograph above. This view is taken from the opposite side (note the railway line on both photos).

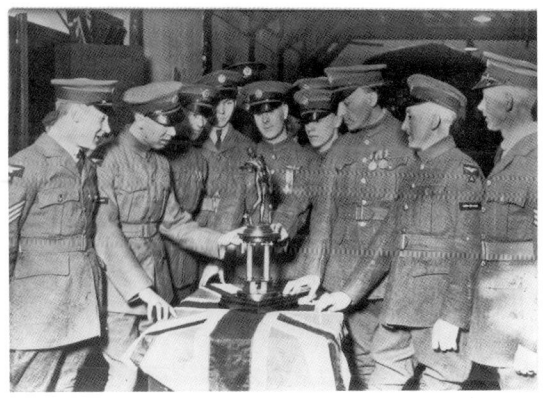

1927: 605 airmen admiring the Lord Esher Trophy, which was awarded annually to the most efficient Auxiliary Squadron. 605 won it 6 times: 1927, 1930, 1931, 1933, 1934 and 1935

Early 1930s: Reg Jones photographed in the air gunners position in Westland Wapiti IIA K1343. Reg took many of the pre-war aerial photographs in this book

Photographs of myself from another plane, taken by my friend Arthur Mobley.

1930: Officers and men with the Lord Esher Trophy; Wapiti IIA in the background at Castle Bromwich

1930: Line-up of Wapitis at Castle Bromwich in readiness for the visit of the Prince of Wales to present the Lord Esher Trophy

4 May 1936: Images of F/Lt Doc Jerome's crashed DH9A J8105, including 2 entries in the Squadron's Rumble Book.

1926: Castle Bromwich aerodrome

1930: Wapiti IIA formation K1136, K1138 & K1141

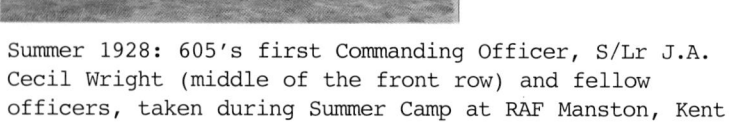

Summer 1928: 605's first Commanding Officer, S/Lr J.A. Cecil Wright (middle of the front row) and fellow officers, taken during Summer Camp at RAF Manston, Kent

Feb 1930: Line-up of Wapitis at Castle Bromwich in readiness for the visit of HRH The Prince of Wales to present the Lord Esher Trophy

Feb 1930: HRH The Prince of Wales (in bowler hat) arriving at Castle Bromwich: CO S/Ldr JAC Wright (3rd left) and F/Lt MacDonald (4th left)

Feb 1930: HRH The Prince of Wales (front row: 4th from the left) with 605 Officers

Early 1930s: Wapiti J9865 after a heavy landing at Castle Bromwich

Early 1930s: A superb line-up of 605 Westland Wapiti II aircraft at Castle Bromwich

1931: Dual Control Avro 504N K1732 at Castle Bromwich

3 Apr 1937: Aerial shot looking towards Minworth, Curdworth and Hams Hall Power Station, North Warwickshire

Christmas 1932: Drill Hall at Castle Bromwich

Summer 1931: German Dornier X Flying boat (D-1929) in Southampton harbour, photographed by 605 airman Reg Jones on a sortie. 605 were on Summer Camp at Manston, Kent at the time.

7 Feb 1931: P/O ES Lambert's Wapiti IIA (possibly J9864), slightly worse for wear after a forced landing near Bristol. According to the Squadron's Rumble Book (below), this incident cost Lambert the princely sum of 17/-.

1931: 605 Officers at Castle Bromwich: L-R: David Lloyd, Tom Beale (killed Sept 41), Colin Barnaby (killed in a collision at C/Brom 9 Dec 34), Mac Goodwin (killed during Battle of Britain with 609 Sqn), Proc Huins, NE Partridge, Baker, "Mac" MacDonald, Eddie Lowe, MV de Satge, Jim Gummow, Gilbert Wright (killed 27 May 40), Doc Jerome, Jim Abell, Walter Churchill (killed 1942).

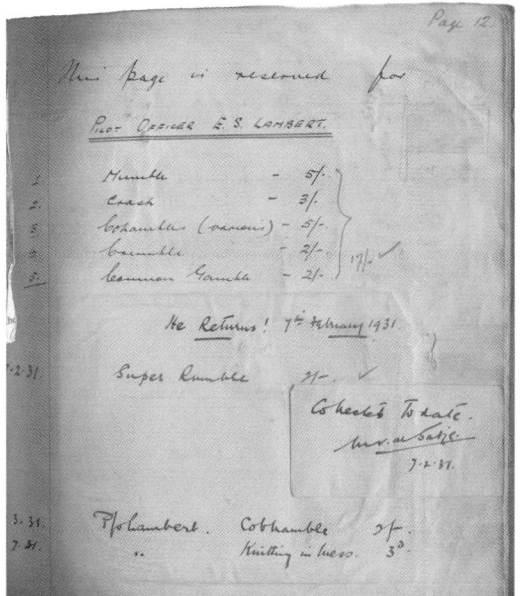

1933: Formation of 605 Wapitis

1936: Tyburn House Island, 2 miles North of the airfield at Castle Bromwich

1930s: Officer's Mess at Castle Bromwich: Note the newspaper-advertising poster above the door, which reads "SLEEP IS JUST A WASTE OF TIME". This was "taken" during a summer camp on the south coast, and was the inspiration for 605's Motto "Nunquam Dormio" – We Never Sleep!

1933: Formation of Wapitis; K1147, J9866, K1343, K1156, K2237, K1146, K1155, K1376, K1367: Note: A copy of this photograph can been seen above the fire place in the photo on the left

1932: Westland Wapiti IIA K1368 at Castle Bromwich

1931: Westland Wapiti IIA K1141 at Castle Bromwich

May 1935: A defining moment in the life of a pilot, "Going Solo". An entry in the log book of P/O Maynard Mitchell (of the famous Midlands Mitchell & Butler brewing company fame). "Mitch" went on to be a great fighter pilot, wining the D.F.C (Distinguished Flying Cross) during the Battle of Britain. The aircraft (Avro K1968) that Mitch went solo in that May day, is pictured left

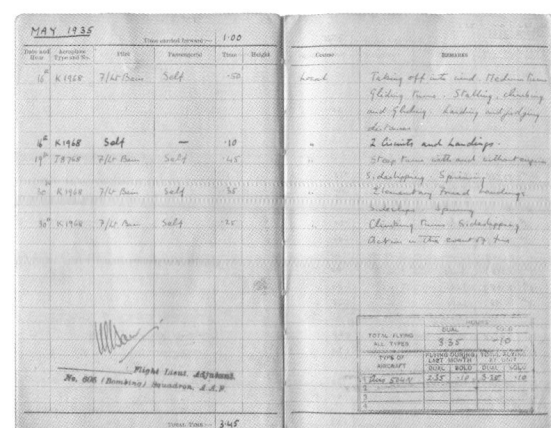

Early 1930s: Avro 504N K1968 at Castle Bromwich

1933: Wapiti K1343: piloted by 605 Commanding Officer, S/Ldr JAC Wright with Air Gunner Pete Wainwright.

1935: The Royal Shakespeare Company's theatre at Stratford-Upon-Avon

Aug 1933: Summer Camp at RAF Manston: Lineup of 501, 605 & 601 Sqaudron Wapitis. The word MANSTON can just be made out ahead of the leading line of aircraft.

1933: Westland Wapiti IIAs K1157, K1155 & K1146

1934: F/Lt S.D. MacDonald D.F.C. (2nd left) and ground crew with Westland Wapiti IIA

1938: RAF Warmwell, taken during 605's Summer Camp

Warwickshire from the air.
These photographs were taken by 605 airman Reg Jones during regular sorties from Castle Bromwich.

16 June 1935: Kenilworth Castle, Warwickshire

June 1934: Coleshill, Warwickshire

1935: Stratford-upon-Avon

1935: Fort Dunlop, Birmingham

25 May 1935: Empire Air Day at Castle Bromwich

25 May 1935: Empire Air Day at Castle Bromwich.
Line-up of 605 Hawker Harts K3892, K3891 & K3890

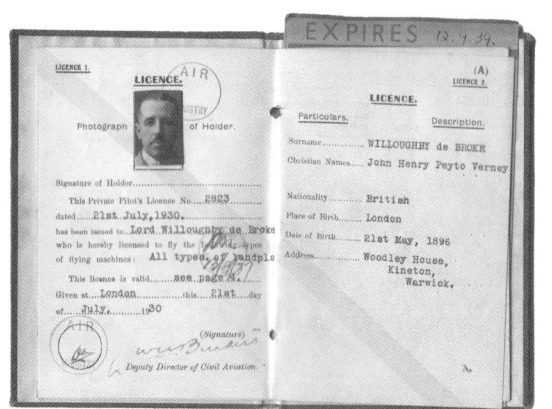

March 1936: Flying License belonging to S/Ldr Lord Willoughby de Broke M.C. A.F.C. who took over command of 605 from S/Ldr JAC Wright in 1936.

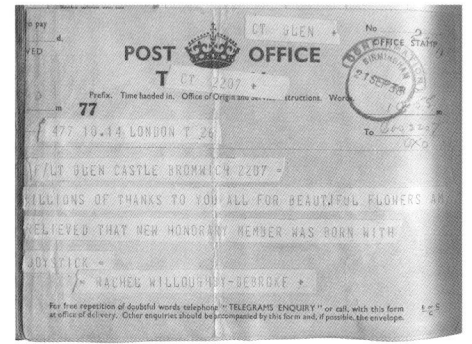

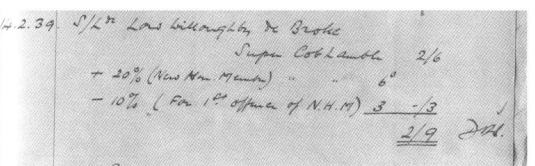

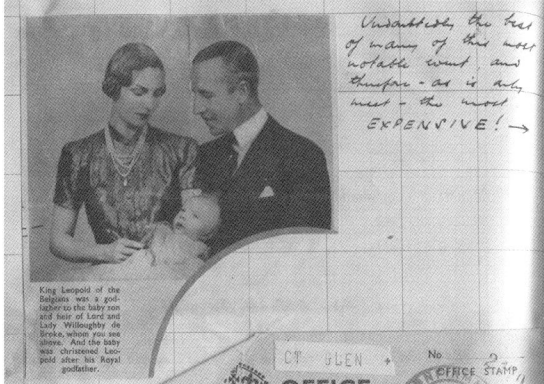

Sept 1938: C/O Lord Willoughby de Broke and his wife Rachel become the proud parents of a new son. Being the Boss didn't exempt you from the "Rumble Book". Lord W, duly fined for "N.H.M." — New Honorary Member.

August 1935: 605 Hawker Harts: K3888, K3877, K3889, K3892, K3891, K3890 & 3 unidentified, photographed over Margate, Kent during the Annual Summer Camp held at nearby Manston. The picture above was taken during the same shoot and was made into a popular postcard.

1936 – Hawker Hinds (K6726, K5533, K5531, K5535, K6676 & 2 others) at Castle Bromwich

August 1936: 605 Airmen enjoying a break in the sunshine during Annual Summer Camp at RAF Aldergrove, Northern Ireland: Hawker Hinds in the background.

August 1935: 605 Hawker Harts K3892, K3891, K3890 over Kent.

1936: 605 Hawker Hart K3891, Hart K1940 (unknown unit), Wapiti in background at Castle Bromwich. Note: flying gear at the ready on the wing.

1937: 605 Rugby Team at Castle Bromwich. Despite much searching of the Squadron archives, no record of their achievement (or lack of it) was found.

1937: AC1 Tommy Glaze posing with a Lewis Gun inside the 605 Armoury at Castle Bromwich. 2 x 250lb and 1 x 500lb bombs

June 1936: 605 take on the might of the City of Birmingham Police in a snooker challenge. F/O Robert Grant-Ferris later became a Tory MP and ended his colourful political career as Lord Harvington.

1937: Hawker Hinds K5540 & K5533 ready to taxi for another sortie.

August 1938: Summer Camp, RAF Warmwell (under canvas!). Standing: Rev McKelvie, F/O Maynard "Mitch" Mitchell, F/O Charlie Thompson, unknown. In chair: F/O Christopher "Jumbo" Deansley. Sitting on grass: F/O Johnny Warren, unknown, F/O Ralph Hope, F/O Denis "Splinters" Smallwood, P/O Graham Austin, P/O Norman Forbes & F/O Pete Danielsen. Johnny Warren was killed after a mid-air collision in Sep 39. Ralph Hope was shot down and killed during the Battle of Britain. Pete Danielsen was killed during the Dunkirk evacuation in May 40. Denis Smallwood (or Splinters as 605 nicknamed him) was a Regular Flying Instructor and had a long and distinguished RAF career. He finally retired as Air Chief Marshal Sir Denis Smallwood GBE KCB DSO DFC. After distinguished careers in the RAF, Graham Austin (who incidentally was "Splinters" first pupil to go solo) was awarded an OBE and AFC, and Mitch and Jumbo were each awarded the DFC (Distinguished Flying Cross).

1932: Visiting Castle Bromwich, Bristol Bulldogs from 23 Squadron. In the cockpit is 23 Sqn CO S/Ldr R.L.R. "Batchy" Atcherley.

Summer 1939: Some of the "boys" at Tangmere: Back row: ?, A/C HV Wild, F/Sgt EF Wild, A/C Bernard Eaton, Cpl Arthur Hadlington, ?,?, LAC Alf Walker, LAC Jones, A/C Jack Pope or Cope. Middle row: A/C Jimmie Grimmett, AC Sid Kimberley, Cpl Bill Bayliss, AC Reynolds, LAC Millward Seated: AC Don Harper, Cpl Les Hubbard.

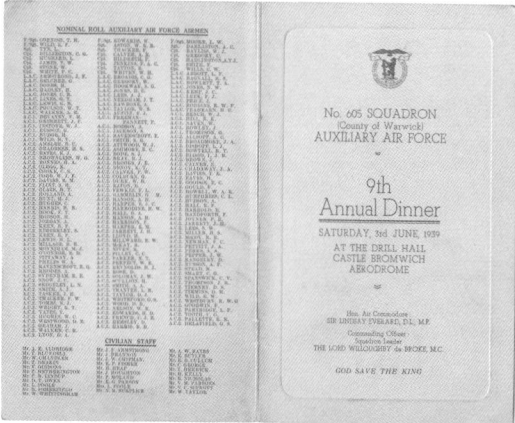

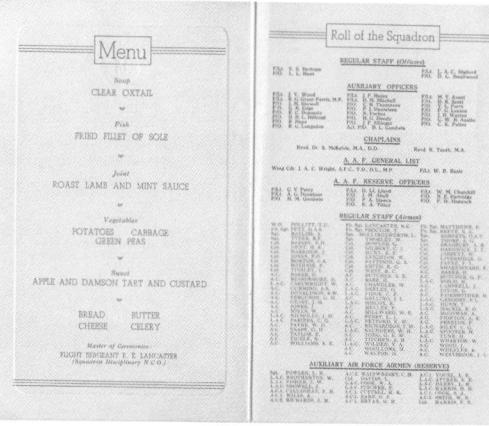

August 1939: 605 Gladiators over RAF Tangmere.

Aug 1939: 605 Gladiatior IIs N5585 (HE-R), N5583 (HE-Q) & N2312 (HE-O) arriving at Tangmere, Sussex for Summer Camp. The Squadron would return to Tangmere several days later after the declaration of War. 605 were accommodated in tents which can be seen in the photo on the left.

August 39: 605 Gladiators over Sussex, operating from Tangmere

19 Sept 39: F/O Norman Forbes with 605 Parachute Packer, Ginger Hodson. Ginger is holding the parachute that Norman used to bail out after his Gladiator collided with another piloted by F/O Johnny Warren. Sadly Johnny was killed.

Summer 39: Gladiator II N5585 HE-R test firing

August 1939: 605 Officers at Tangmere, L-R: P/O Graham Doody, F/O Pat Leeson, F/Lt Walter Churchill, F/O Norman Forbes, F/O Peter Danielsen, F/O Douglas Scott, F/Lt "Proc" Huins, F/Lt Maynard Mitchell, F/O Charlie Thompson & F/Lt Mark Avent

August 1939: 605's first Hawker Hurricane Mk I, L1830, which was delivered to Tangmere during Summer Camp.

Sep 1939: F/Lt Pat Leeson with his Hurricane. Note the per-war HE code. Pat, who was a very popular pilot, was shot down and captured over Dunkirk in May 1940. After two audacious escapes, Pat was sent to Stalag Luft III and was involved in the infamous mass break out that became known as "The Great Escape".

Aug 1939: 605 officers relaxing outside the Officer's Mess at Tangmere. L-R: F/O Brian Hillcoat (standing), F/O Ralph Hope, F/O Johnny Warren (standing), F/O Jumbo Deansley, I/O ? and 2 unidentified. Brian, Ralph and Johnny were killed during the War.

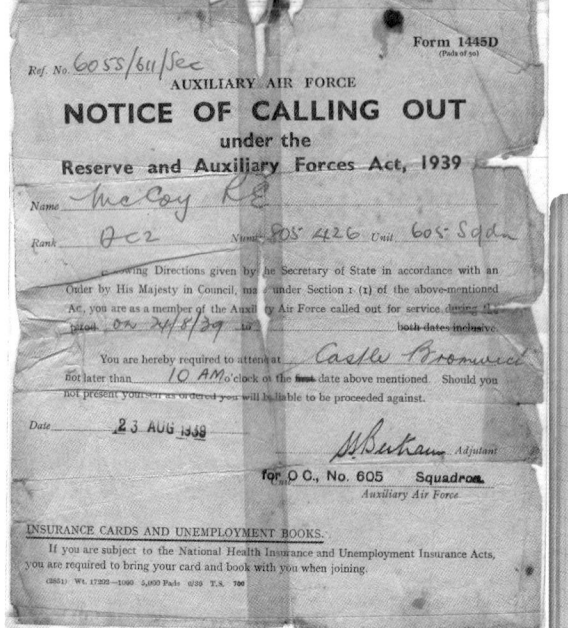

23 Aug 1939: 805426 AC2 Richard McCoy's Calling Out card

3 Sept 1939: WAR! The entry in F/Lt Maynard Mitchell's log-book speaks for itself

8 July 1939: 605 take part in the official opening of Elmdon (Birmingham) Airport.

Feb 1940: 605 Pilots, billeted in McKays Hotel, Wick: F/O Brian Hillcoat (killed Oct 40), F/O Carter, F/O Bunny Currant, F/O Graham Austin, F/O Pete Danielsen (killed May 40) & F/O Grant-Ferris. Note the "Sleep Is A Waste Of Time" poster on the right. See page 17.

Feb 1940: Not one of ours! Crashed No.111 Squadron Hurricane JU-?. 605 was sharing Wick with 111 at the time.

Mar 1940: 605 ground personnel with Hurricane UP-M at Wick

Scotland in the Snow, Wick Feb 1940: 605 Hurricanes running their engines, which they were required to do owing to the extreme cold conditions.

Mar 1940: F/O Pete Danielsen and F/O Graham Austin at Wick. Both men were shot down 2 months later during the evacuation of Dunkirk. Sadly Pete was killed and his body was never recovered. Graham was badly injured and bailed out over Dunkirk. Fortunately he landed over Allied territory and returned to Newhaven via a Hospital Ship.

Feb 1940: Luftwaffe He.111 which force-landed at Wick one night. The crew were so disoriented that they believed they were landing on water and even threw life-rafts from the aircraft.

Aug 1939: 605 Squadron Band at Tangmere
Back row (L-R): Don Wood, Sid Cook*
Middle row (L-R): Ginger Hodson*, Alf Perks*, Curly Lewis*, Jack Graham*, Harry Stead, Brummie Naven*, Bernard Eaton, George Thompson*, Les Dangerfield, Ernie Perfect, Alf Lees.
Front Row (L-R): Sid Lees, Les Sedgeley, Cliff Hughes, Wally Bench, S/Ldr Lord Willoughby de Broke, Tommy Wills, Bill Cobb, Chick Jordon, Charlie Amber*

Nine members of the band (marked *) were captured by the Japanese in Feb 1942, Alf Perks and were Charlie Ambler were killed.

Feb 1940: 605 Hurricane UP-M at Wick

Feb 1940: Victor Ransom with Hurricane UP-J

Feb 1940: 605 pilots at Wick

Feb 1940: 605 pilots at Wick: F/Lt Gerry Edge in tunic on the left

605: OUR FEW

S/Ldr Walter Churchill D.S.O. D.F.C.

F/O Mike Cooper-Slipper D.F.C.

F/Lt Bunny Currant D.F.C.

F/Lt Gerry Edge D.F.C.

P/O Charles English (KIA 7 Oct 1940)

P/O Bob Foster

F/O James "Spud" Hayter

P/O Alec Ingle

P/O Eric Jones

P/O S.J. Madle

Sgt Peter McIntosh (KIA 12 Oct 1940)

S/Ldr Archie McKellar D.F.C. (KIA 1 Nov 1940)

P/O Archie Milne

P/O "Jock" Muirhead D.F.C. (KIA 15 Oct 1940)

Sgt Raimund Puda (Czech)

F/O Peter Parrott D.F.C. The above photograph was used in an RAF recruiting poster.

Sgt Dougle Ritchie
(KIA 9 Aug 1940)

5 April 1941: P/O EJ "Watty" Watson, F/O Price (I/O), F/Lt Gerry Edge DFC, F/O Graham Austin, F/O Basil Friendship DFM & F/O Cyril Passy at Graham Austin's Wedding

Sgt Charles Soans

Sgt Ken Jones (on right) with one of 605's two Polish pilots, either Sgt Budzinski or P/O Glowacki in one of the gardens at Foresters Drive, Croydon

P/O Peter Thompson

Sgt L.F. Ralls

1990: 605's Battle of Britain 50th Anniversary Dinner. Back row: W/Cdr Bunny Currant DSO DFC & Bar, Ken Jones (ex-POW), W/Cdr Bob Foster DFC, S/Ldr Mike Cooper-Slipper DFC
Front Row: F/Lt Archie Milne, G/Cpt Alec Ingle DFC AFC, G/Cpt Gerry Edge OBE DFC, W/Cdr Jack Fleming, W/Cdr Peter Parrott DFC & Bar, AFC

Oct 1940: 605 ground-crews re-arming and refuelling Hurricane UP-M at Croydon

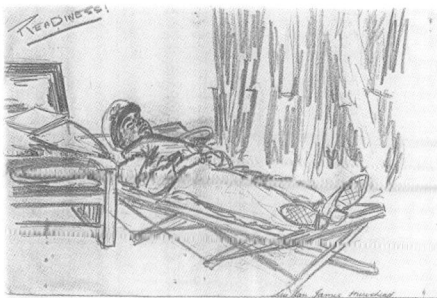 

Summer 1940: 2 sketches by Ian 'Jock' Muirhead. The image on the right is 'B' Flight Commander F/Lt. Archie McKellar. Both men were killed during the Battle of Britain.

1968: Sir Lawrence Olivier and W/Cdr Lord Willoughby de Broke on the set of the epic film "Battle Of Britain". Sir Lawrence played Air Chief Marshal Lord Dowding Commander-in-Chief Fighter Command in the film. Lord Willoughby was Senior Sector Controller at Kenley during the Battle. Right, a letter from AVM Keith Park, AOC No.11 Group to Lord Willoughby.

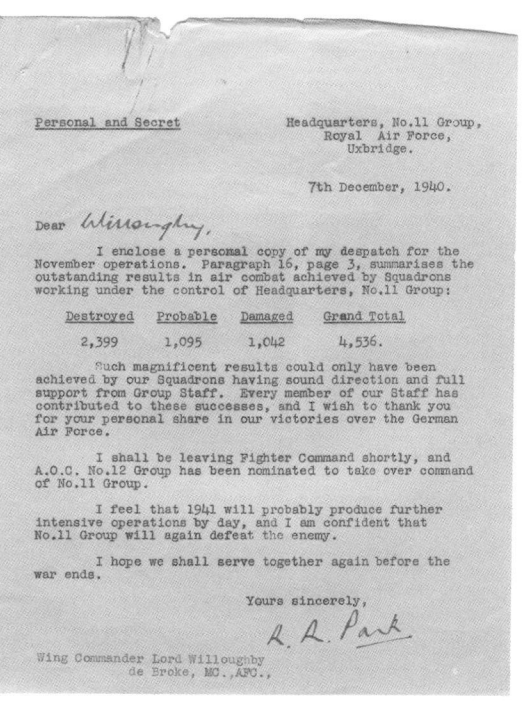

Sept 1940: Friends and Luftwaffe Me.109 pilots, Uffz Paul Lederer and Uffz Paul Lege at a German airfield in France. Both men where shot down by 605 on 7/10/40, Lederer was killed and Lege was captured. Paul Lege wrote to the author seeking his help in finding the grave of his friend.

1940: 605 Hurricane UP-U at Croydon

Oct 1940: F/Sgt Jenkins watching one of the many dog-fights involving 605, that took place over Croydon during the Battle of Britain.

Sept 1940: 605 Intelligence Officer, F/Lt Hutton at Croydon: Hurricane UP-A in the background.

1940 - Cliff's Crotchets, 605 Dance Band, Croydon: Cliff Hughes - Piano, Ginger Hodson & Dick Etty - Saxaphone, 2 trumpeters-names forgotten, Jack Graham - Thombone, Ken Swann - Drums & Sgt Shakespeare at the mike)

Sept 1940: Four Friends. These three photographs (right) were taken during the height of the Battle of Britain, in the gardens of houses in Forester's Drive, Croydon that was used to billet 605. All four were posted overseas with 605 and arrived in Java, Feb 1941. A few days later the Squadron was overrun and attacked by Japanese paratroopers. Bill Kelly & Freddie Dowding were killed.

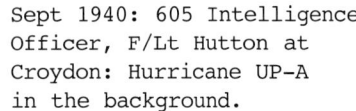

Bill Kelly: Despite being unarmed, Bill was shot in the stomach by a Japanese soldier and killed.

George Jones

Norman Connew and Freddie Dowding: Norman was badly hurt by Japanese gunfire, and despite his own appalling injuries, his life was saved by George Jones.

Sept 1940: Mike Cooper-Slipper's Hurricane L2012 at Croydon. On 15/9/40 during a frantic dog-fight over Kent, Mike ran out of ammo and decided to ram a Do.17. He brought down the Hun and was thrown clear and parachuted to safety. (see page 4)

Oct 1940: Hurricane UP-M at Croydon

Jan 1941: Engineering Officer F/Lt Jimmy Addison, on the good ship "Isobella" at Woodbridge. The ship was home for some of 605's officers.

Aug 1941: 605 airmen in Leamington Spa

Aug 1941: Ernie Currill and 605 Mascot, Raff at Honiley

Jul 1941: 605 airmen at Baginton, Coventry. Front row (L-R): Ernie Currill, A. Dalgarno, Stan Annis, Tiny Morris & Tich Hornsby.

Jun 1941: ?, Bill Bridges, Jerry Kucera (Czech), Tommy Cornish, Pat Hubbard, Phillip Wigley, Les Tye & Sonny Ormrod at Ternhill

Oct 1941: W/O Tommy Cornish, A/Cdr Sir Lindsay Everard, W/Cdr Lord Willoughby de Broke at Honiley

Honiley 1941: ?, ?, Ken Dawick, Thompson, Joe Beckett

Oct 1941: 605 at Honiley, in what became a "farewell" photo as the Squadron were posted overseas shortly afterwards.

Oct 1941: 605 Honorary Air Commodore Sir Lindsay Everard with S/Ldr Reid inspecting 605 at Honiley

Oct 1941: W/Cdr Lord Willoughby de Broke being shown the cockpit of one of 605's Hurricanes at Honiley

Late 41: Sonny Ormrod, Ron Noble & Joe Beckett in Malta

Late 41: Ian MacKay, Ron Noble & Chuck Lester in Malta

Nov 1941: 605 Hurricane Mk.II BG753 UP-V in Malta. Ron Noble had flown this aircraft off the Ark Royal 12/11/41

Late 41: Peter Lowe, George Allen, Chuck Lester, Ian MacKay & Phil Wigley in Malta

1942: Far East

1942: Hurricanes aboard HMS Indomitable, heading for the Far East.

Jan 1942: Servicing a Hurricane at Palembang, Java

Jan 1942: Hurricane at Palembang, Java

Early 1942: Tjillilitan airfield, Java

Feb 1942: 605 personnel trying to escape from the advancing Japanese Army. Engineering Officer F/Lt Jimmy Addison is standing next to the carriage on the right

Feb 1942: After the fall of Singapore, 605 personnel in Java were captured by the Japanese. A large group were sent to the shipyard at Habu, Japan

Feb 1942: Another view of the dockyard at Habu, Japan

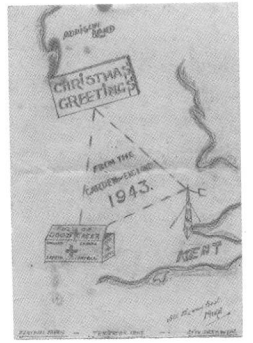

FEPOW (Far East Prisoner Of War): Some hand made Christmas cards sent to Jimmy Addison. Despite their optimism Christmas 1943, they had to endure a further 2 1/2 years of captivity. Sadly many never made it.

May 1945: The nightmare is over. Some of the 605 lads, after 3 1/2 years as Prisoners of War

May 1945: Tokyo Bay, Japan

1945 — Ex-FEPOWs leaving Yokohama, Japan aboard the escort carrier H.M.S. Ruler, bound for Australia.

DUKE OF GLOUCESTER GREETS P.o.W.

WHEN 30 men of 605 County of Warwick Auxiliary Squadron arrived recently at Sydney en route for England from Japan, where they had been prisoners of war, they were greeted by H.R.H. the Duke of Gloucester, Governor-General of Australia.

All the men looked fit and well, and when they reach the United Kingdom arrangements will be made to hold a squadron reunion in their honour.

News of the Duke's gesture towards the men reached London in a special cable from Brigadier Schreiber, the Chief of Staff to His Royal Highness.

It was addressed to Air Commodore Lord Willoughby de Broke, Director of Public Relations, Air Ministry, and a former Commanding Officer of the squadron, who sent the following reply:—

"Most grateful your cable re 605 Squadron ex-P.o.W., which I read out to-day to gathering of 605 Auxiliary officers in London. They asked me to express my warmest thanks to H.R.H. for his message and would be grateful if you would convey their cordial greetings to 605 ex-P.o.W. from Japan and say their return is anxiously awaited and that a squadron reunion will then be arranged. Grateful also if you could forward nominal roll giving home addresses, with any relevant information concerning other 605 P.o.W."

The County of Warwick Squadron, of which the returning men are members, was formed at Castle Bromwich in 1926, and, before going to the Far Eastern theatre of operations, had built up a formidable record in combat, having destroyed 167 enemy aircraft, probably destroyed 28, and damaged more than 130 others.

The squadron claimed its first Hun in 1940 while countering enemy attacks on Scapa Flow, and in the same year helped to cover the Dunkirk evacuation. The squadron was at Croydon for the Battle of Britain. During September and October, 1940, its pilots destroyed more than 40 enemy aircraft, probably destroyed 15, and damaged another 40 for the loss of six of their own aircraft.

In the following year they operated in defence of Malta, suffering great losses. The squadron was re-formed back in England in 1942 to attack targets in France, take part in many intruder patrols, and escort bombers to heavily defended targets. No. 605 left Fighter Command in November, 1944, to join the Second Tactical Air Force, and, flying Mosquitoes, harassed German communications.

Its members also destroyed 75 flying bombs.

Feb 42 : Group of captured 605 airmen, photographed by the Japanese Imperial Army. This photograph was taken from the Jap offices by the survivors in 45.

June 1942: By the end of February 1942, 605 personnel in the Far East had been captured by the Japanese, and the majority of our pilots in Malta had become part of No. 185 Squadron. It was decided to reform 605 under the command of the legendry fighter pilot, W/Cdr Peter Townsend D.S.O. D.F.C.

W/Cdr. P.W. Townsend. D.S.O.,D.F.C., Officer Commanding from 7th. June 1942 to 7th. August 1942.

THE Peter Townsend !!

Details of the first operational sortie by the re-formed 605 Squadron extracted from the Operations Record Book (Form 540).

FORD. 14/7/42. First operational trip carried out by Squadron. W/Cdr. Townsend (Pilot), P/O Palmer (Observer. 23 Sqdn.), Sgt. Wiseman (A.G.), took off in a Havoc 1 at 23.59 hours to bomb CAEN Marshalling Yards. 1/250 lb. bomb(inst), 1/250 lb. bomb(½ delay) and 12/40 lb bombs (inst), dropped at 0108 hours from 2,000 feet on sidings west of Mandeville power station east of canal and west of river Orne. Bomb burst were felt but not seen owing to light flak behind.
Crossed French coast at CARBOUGG at 3,000 feet at 0038 hours. Beacons seen at Fecamp, Le Havre, Trouville, W. of river Orne and one very bright further west in direction of Pt. de la PERCHE. 2 searchlights from Le Havre tried to illuminate.
Arrived target area at 0055 hours and ran up from East to West but overshot - slight inaccurate flak and two searchlights - orbited, then ran up from South to North and bombed. Narrow beam searchlight with red light beside pointed in direction of Havoc, shining on and then off with a horizontal beam. Havoc re-crossed French coast at mouth of River Orne at 2,500 feet at 0110 hours and landed at base at 0210 hours.
Weather was good over channel deteriorating slightly over French coast, patches of low cloud forming at 1,000 feet. Visibility good.

Note :- At this stage the Squadron had only five aircraft and the next day's entry in the F.540 refers to the arrival of the 6th. Havoc.

Nov. 24th. 1942 at Ford.
The Air Officer Commanding No.11 Group presented the Squadron Badge and took the salute on 24/11/42. The A.O.C., Air Marshall T. Leigh-Mallory, C.B., D.S.O., can be seen in the front row with the Commanding Officer, W/Cdr. G.L.Denholm, D.F.C., seated on his left.

Seated left to right: P/O Moore, P/O Peill, P/O Green, P/O Battle, F/Lt. Cubitt, F/Lt. Olley, F/Lt. Mack, W/Cdr. G.C.Maxwell, M.C.,D.F.C.,A.F.C., G/Capt. H.D.McGregor, D.S.O., Air Marshall T. Leigh-Mallory, C.B.,D.S.O., W/Cdr. G.L.Denholm,D.F.C., S/Ldr. C.D. Tomalin, A.F.C., F/Lt. Maggs, F/Lt. Hindle, P/O Pensford, P/O Smart, P/O Weed, P/O May. (The following were later awarded D.F.C's:- Mack, Tomalin, Maggs, Hindle, Pensford, Smart and Weed. Olley was later awarded the A.F.C.,).

1st. Row standing left to right: Sgt. Stirrat, Sgt. Hedson, Sgt. Edwards, F/Sgt. Howse, Sgt. Devine, Sgt. Cakebread, Sgt. Gray, Sgt. Harvey, Sgt. Martin, F/Sgt. Andersen, Sgt. Rudd, Sgt. Linn (later D.F.C.,), P/O Richards, P/O Sutcliffe, P/O J. Mills, P/O Michie, P/O Hedder (later D.F.C.,), P/O Muir (later D.F.C.,), Sgt. Hinsworth, Sgt. Smith, M.G.M., Sgt. Haley, Sgt. Collins.

Back Row left to right: Sgt. Brochocki, Sgt. James, Sgt. Johns, Sgt. Weed, Sgt. Hine, Sgt. Harrison (later D.F.C.,), Sgt. Wimpenny, Sgt. Vipond, Sgt. Penny.

Warrant Officer G.W. Lydiatt.

Arriving shortly after 605 re-formed, W/O Lydiatt, Fitter Armourer, remained with the Squadron and was there when they disbanded. Throughout these four years he rendered magnificent service to 605 and the Armament Section, of which he was N.C.O. i/c, was always a most efficient part of "The Fighting 605th". Especially was this so during the months with No. 2 Group, when the understaffed armourers were hard pressed and overworked.

Winter 1942: 605 Boston

Some 'B' Flight Aircrew by one of their Bostons at Ford, Sussex in Feb.1943.
Left to right;- P/O D.L.Moore, P/O J.Sutcliffe, P/O D.May, Sgt. W.Harrison, S/Ldr. A.W.Mack, F/O R.Smart, F/O C.F.Ponsford, P/O P.D.J.Wood.
Out of this group six were later decorated for their services with the Squadron;- F/O Wood & F/O Smart were awarded D.F.C's in July 1943, S/Ldr Mack a D.F.C. in Sept 1943, F/O Sutcliffe was Mentioned, W/O Harrison a D.F.C. in June 1945 and S/Ldr Ponsford was awarded the D.F.C. in Sept 1945.

F/O R.R.Smart with his navigator, F/O J.K.Sutcliffe.
This crew were posted to the Squadron from 51 O.T.U. Cranfield on 19th Aug. 1942. They successfully completed a tour of operations by Aug.1943 when they left the Squadron. F/O Ray Smart had then destroyed 4 e/a and probably destroyed another and had been awarded the D.F.C., in July. He did not go to O.T.U. for a 'rest' period but 'pressed on' with Ops and was unfortunately later reported missing from a night sortie with F.I.U.

The Squadron Operations Room at Ford. (Feb. '43)
Left to right;- Sgt. J.W.Tredwen.(later W/O and 'Mention', completed 59 sorties with 605), P/O H.C.Muir.(later F/Lt and D.F.C.,), Sgt. A.Chilton.(missing 25/26th May '43), Sgt. P. N. Napper, Sgt. G.B.Wait, Sgt. D.A.W. Norton, Sgt. E.J.Harvey.(back to camera), F/Sgt ?.

31 Dec 42: 605 lost a very popular all-Scotish crew on the last day of 42 when their Boston crashed near Ford returning from an Op: Sgt James Warrender (Pilot), Sgt Robert Veitch (Observer) & Sgt James Stirrat (Wireless/Air Gunner)

S/Ldr. A.G.Woods, D.F.C., and Bar, with his navigator F/O W.H.Johnson,D.F.C.,D.F.M.
"Get up them stairs!"

This crew arrived on the Squadron in March '43, as Flying Officer and Sergeant respectfully. It took them a little time to live down their second ops trip when owing to an intermittent electrical short on the gun wiring system they had to make several attacks on a He 111 before they could get the guns to fire and hit it. The short not being discovered for some time it was commonly alleged that the pilot had given the Hun hods of brake pressure instead of shells by pressing the brake lever (Lhewl) of the gun button. Another theory had it that he was using the camera gun and was not really offensively minded!!

After this they had some 'joy' on occasions and when they finished their first tour in Jan '44 they had destroyed two E/A, probably destroyed a third and damaged three. In March they were awarded the D.F.C., and D.F.M., respectively and they spent their six months 'rest' instructing at O.T.U.

In July '44, they returned to the Squadron as Flight Lieutenant and Pilot Officer, Wilf Johnson having been commissioned from F/Sgt. during his 'rest'. They managed to talk the C.O. into letting them do the odd daylight trip, but apart from severely damaging a 900 ton tanker off Norway and destroying a 'diver' when returning from one trip, they had little success. However it brought the daylight possibilities to the front and got the Squadron interested - the interest being well illustrated by the record results obtained in October doing daylight rangers.

In Feb '45, F/Lt. Woods was appointed 'B' Flight Commander and made Acting Squadron Leader and after W/Cdr Mitchell went missing in March '45, he commanded the Squadron until W/Cdr Horne arrived near the end of April. By the end of the war in Europe, this crew had completed over 75 sorties and a little later were awarded a Bar to the D.F.C., and the D.F.C., respectfully. Both remained with 605 and S/Ldr. Woods was Acting C.O. when the Squadron disbanded and took over a new number, W/Cdr. Horne having been posted a few weeks earlier.

March 43: S/Ldr Arthur Woods D.F.C., firing a "loaned" Colt 45.

P/O D.W.C.Wood and F/O P.D.J.Wood.
This crew joined 605 on the 14th July 1942 as Sgt. and P/O respectively. Sgt. Dudley Wood was commissioned in April 1943, & in July 1943 F/O Peter Wood was awarded the D.F.C. Both successfully completed their tour of Operations and were posted in Sept and Nov. 1943 respectively. F/O Dudley Wood was later reported missing from Operations with 515 Squadron.
On the night of the 11/12th June 1943 they destroyed an e/a at Gilze/Rijen and the following is extracted from the Combat Report.
".........left Castle Camps at 23.19 hours.....landfall at Westhoofd at 00.01 ......reached target at 00.12.....V/1 alight..... about one minute after arrival an e/a was seen burning navigating lights flying over flare-path.......we turned to attack....e/a doused nav lights and was lost......continued patrol......second e/a seen travelling across wind about to turn down the visual lorenz.....opened up to 300mph.......followed down the visual lorenz losing height........at 3/400 feet above ground and approx. 250 yards behind I gave him a 1-1½ second burst, the e/a then being about 500 yards from the end of the runway......strikes along the port wing and fuselage and he continued at a steeper angle of approach with navigation lights still burning and at 00.28 hours crashed at end of runway..... as he hit there was an explosion and his navigation lights went out......continued patrol......saw third e/a burning nav. lights...as he approached he was given a red and I turned to attack he doused lights...... 2 S/L's coming up and appeared to 'home' him to Eindhoven........continued patrol til 01.12 hours.....crossed out Westhoofd at 01.19."

May 1943: Mosquito Mk II DZ716 UP-L at Castle Camps, preparing to start engines and head off into the night on another Intruder sortie.

S/Ldr. D.H.Blomeley D.F.C. - F/O R.Birrell (later D.F.C.) with their Mosquito and ground crew, L.A/C Richards (fitter), L.A/C Garver (rigger).

'Blom' and 'Jock' were posted to the Squadron on the 5th. April 1943 and soon made a name for themselves. 'Blom' was an 'old hand' and had previously served with 151 Sqdn at North Weald and later with 607 Sqdn. at Deanl; he was reputed to have destroyed 10 huns with 607 during the period 17th May to 12th. July 1940, but as the Sqdn records had been lost in France this was not confirmed. However he was known to have been shot down in June '40 over the enemy lines. He baled out, evaded capture and returned to his unit some days later. He arrived on the Squadron a F/Lt. and was promoted to Acting Squadron Leader on 12th. Oct '43 by which time he had destroyed four more huns and had been awarded the D.F.C., Jock Birrell navigated him on all his sorties and when 'Blom' was posted in Feb '44, Jock crewed up with his successor as 'B' Flight Commander, S/Ldr Carver (later D.F.C.,). Together they destroyed 3 Pilotless aircraft and in May '44, Jock was promoted Acting F/Lt. and appointed Squadron Navigation Officer. Later in '44 he was awarded the D.F.C., and in September he was posted away.

'Blom' and Jock's victims were all far from sitting birds. The first was an Me 109 which jumped them in moonlight near Jagel on 17th Aug. '43 - a dogfight ensued and 'Blom' won - no mean feat in a Mossie. The next were two Ju 88's in daylight over the Skagerrak in Sept '43 and in Nov. '43 he shot down an Me110 which came up to intercept him at Aalborg, Denmark in foul weather, also in daylight.

Copies of all three combat reports are given here.

1943: F/Lt Mike Olley A.F.C.

F/Lt. C.E.Knowles. D.F.C., and Bar with his navigator F/O A.R.Eagling.
Posted to 605 on the 5th. April '43, F/Lt. Clive Knowles had already completed 83 sorties with P.R.U. and had been awarded the D.F.C., Alan Eagling was a P/O and was new to Operations. They joined 'A'Flight and made an excellent crew, F/Lt. Knowles later becoming Deputy Flight Commander. Completing 30 sorties they destroyed 3 enemy aircraft at night and carried out numerous bombing attacks on the enemy's main airfields in Germany, Holland, France and Belgium. F/Lt. Knowles was awarded a Bar to his D.F.C., for his work with the Squadron.
The following is extracted from a combat report referring to the night of 25/26th July 1943:- "......Mosquito UP/A took off at 0107 hours from Castle Camps to intrude on returning enemy minelayers at Soesterburg........landfall made at Overflakke at 0150 hours.....target area reached at 0210 hours where the M/S V/L was seen to be alight and a white beacon flashing "ZW" was seen to the S of the A/D ......after 10 minutes patrol saw aircraft lights on far side of drome.... unable to make contact.....15 minutes later two e/a were seen making their approach from the north, burning Red-White recognition lights.....hinder one doused his lights shortly after and we dived on the first......I gave a 3 second burst of cannon and machine gun from 350 yards closing to 50 yards, from astern and above using 5 degrees deflection at 1500 feet......saw strikes on port engine and fuselage.... burst into flames.....we recognised it to be a Do 217 and we saw the hood jettison ....we broke away to port and saw the e/a crash to the east of the aerodrome at 0230 hours......During our dive and combat, and until breaking away we were held by a searchlight on the line of the Lorenz at the north end and by others round this end of the A/D, and were engaged by flak from the A/D defences......A/D lights doused and we continued our patrol until 0245 hours.... crossed out Overflakke.... landed base 0348 hours".

W/Cdr. C.D.Tomalin. D.F.C.,A.F.C., Officer Commanding from 1st. May 1943 to 25th. Sept. 1943. Previously commanded 'A' Flight from 22nd. Nov. 1942. Awarded D.F.C., in October 1943;- citation reads,"He has shown a fine example of leadership, and his first consideration has been the operational efficiency of crews under his command; ....He has at all times shown an excellent example of determination and has been an inspiration to aircrew serving under him.

Two crews being briefed by the 'Met Man' in the Ops Room at Castle Camps in May '43. Left to right:- Sgt. E.G.M.Smith (Pilot), Sgt. E.J.Harvey (Pilot), Sgt. A. Chilten (Nav), Sgt. G.B.Wait (Nav) and the 'Met Man'. Smith and Chilten failed to return from a sortie on the night of the 25th/26th. May 1943.

Page 2.—THE DAILY SKETCH, FRIDAY, MAY 21, 1943

'INTRUDERS' SCARE AWAY RAIDERS

By 'Daily Sketch' Correspondent, R.A.F. Fighter Station, Somewhere in England, Thursday.

R.A.F. "intruders" — the Mosquitoes which attack German bombers as they try to land at their bases after carrying out raids on Britain — are inflicting incredibly high losses on enemy air strength.

And they help to keep the Luftwaffe from bombing this country.

So harassed are the Germans by our persistent "intruders" that, when they know Mosquitoes are in the vicinity they direct their returning bombers to other bases.

Unable To Land

Frequently the Mosquitoes' operations are so widespread that the enemy machines are "turned down" by base after base.

They cannot get permission to land anywhere. In the end, they run out of petrol and crash.

These Mosquitoes also cover our own bomber operations. And they are "train-busters" too—in their spare time.

In six months this squadron, which fought in France, in the Battle of Britain, and in defence of Singapore, has destroyed five enemy aircraft, probably destroyed one and damaged five; destroyed two locomotives, damaged 48, and damaged two barges.

Their successes, however, are far greater than is conveyed by mere figures.

Most Patient Job

The commander of the squadron, Wing-Commander C. D. Tomalin, A.F.C., who is a former Olympic high-diving champion, told me that theirs was the most patient job in the Royal Air Force.

"We hang round the German bases," he said, "until either we spot something or our time is up.

"Sometimes German aircraft have crashed because we have been covering their bases, and we know that, we are responsible for the destruction of far more planes than we claim.

"There is no doubt that 'intruder' operations are having a great effect on German night flying and German morale."

F/O K.H. Smart watches three navigators prepare for the night's work. Castle Camps. May '43. Left to right the three are:- F/O J.K.Sutcliffe, F/O P.D.J.Wood, F/O D.May.

May 1943: 605 aircrew at Castle Camps before an Intruder sortie: F/Lt Brain Williams on left

Summer 1943:
Four 605 MkII
deHavilland Mosquito
heading towards the
Dutch coast (L-R:
DZ691; DZ717; DZ724
UP-S; DZ716 UP-L)

F/Lt. W.A.Bird, D.F.C., and F/Lt. L.H.Hodder, D.F.C.,
Les Hodder joined the Squadron as a P/O shortly after it reformed and was Colin Ponsford's
navigator until Feb.'43 when he was detached to 157 Squadron where he acted as Nav. Off.
and flew with the C.O. He returned to 605 in May '43 as an Acting F/Lt. and flew with
S/Ldr. Gibbs. D.F.C., before crewing up with Dickie Bird who had recently arrived with
a navigator who was U/S for flying. This was in Aug.'43 and the partnership continued
successfully until June '44, when Dickie was posted on completion of his 2nd. tour of
Ops. His first tour had been with 23 Squadron, the pioneer Intruders where he had some
success. With 605, they destroyed one Hun and damaged another and in May '44 were both
awarded the D.F.C. 'Les had then completed over 50 sorties and so had Dickie, and they
made an inspiring crew. As Squadron Navigation Officer, Les worked like a nigger and
no-one deserved more his promotion to Squadron Leader on posting from the Squadron on
the 26th. April '44.

F/O R.L.Williams (Southern Rhodesia) with his navigator, F/O F.E.Hogg. D.F.C., Croix de
Guerre (New Zealand).
This crew were posted to 605 Squadron on the 28th. Sept 1943. F/O 'Leo' Williams
had already completed a very successful tour of Intruder Operations with 23 Squadron and
had 3 enemy aircraft destroyed to his credit. 'Frankie' Hogg had completed two tours of
Operations - one with Bomber Command and the second with 418 Squadron, our Canadian
rival home-based Intruder Squadron. During this second tour, he was awarded the D.F.C.,
They soon made a name for themselves with 605 and by the end of March 1944, they
had destroyed 2 and damaged a further six enemy aircraft all at night. Leo Williams was
then awarded the D.F.C., and in May 1944, this crew split up when Frankie Hogg was
repatriated to New Zealand. F/O Hogg was awarded a Bar to his D.F.C., about this time.
F/O Williams carried on operating and did a number of trips with F/O 'Stan' Hatsell
navigating. By the end of June this team had destroyed 3, probably destroyed 1, and
damaged four enemy aircraft, which brought Leo's personal score to at least 8 ; 1 ; 12.
Classified as Tour Expired, F/Lt Williams was posted from 605 on the 9th July '44,
but refusing to 'rest', he went to F.I.U., and then 501 Squadron which had just formed
up with Tempests where he reaped further joy against the hun pilotless aircraft. And
so to F.E.F. where on Daylight Rangers after more joy he finally 'failed to return'.
This was shortly after he had been awarded a Bar to his D.F.C.,
On leaving the Squadron in July 1944, F/Lt. Williams had completed 80 operational
sorties. With so many combat reports to choose from it is rather a job to select one to
quote briefly here especially as he flew with two navigators so I have selected two
reports; the first for the 19th. Feb'44 when F/O R.L.Williams and F/O F.E.Hogg went to
patrol Brussels/Melsbroek and Le Culot airfields.

June 1943: Mosquito MkII DZ716 UP-L

Oct 1943: Ops Room at Bradwell Bay; L-R: S/Ldr A Mack, F/O "Fairey" Battle (I/O) on phone, F/Lt ? (on phone), F/O Bob Muir, C/O W/Cdr Charles Tomalin, F/O Brian Williams, P/O Dudley Wood, P/O JK Sutcliffe, F/O Ray Smart, F/O Peter Wood, F/O Dougie May

Sgt. A.T.Linn and F/O D.May. Photographs taken in June 1943 at Castle Camps, Cambs. This crew successfully completed a tour with 605 from August 1942 to Nov. 1943 during which time they destroyed a Do-217 and an Me 210 at night. One photo shows them examining repair work in progress on their aircraft following the previous night's Op in which they destroyed the 210. A bird had holed the starboard leading edge of the Mosquito's wing.
The following is extracted from the combat report:-
"....took off from Castle Camps at 00.08 hours.....landfall at Overflakke at 00.51......target reached at 0132......patrol was made N,S and W of the aerodrome until at 01.55 hours while on the west side of Venlo at 800 feet an e/a with a single white light was sighted to port...... while we were still climbing the e/a turned.....we came astern..... e/a burning white wing-tip lights......about 4 miles NW of Venlo we closed to 150 yards and reducing speed to 150 mph indicated I gave a 1½ second burst closing to 50 yards....strikes on the starboard engine which caught fire and crashed almost immediately at 0159 hours....recognised the e/a as an Me 210 by the shape of the tail unit silhouetted against the fire.....we exposed the camera gun for 5 secs on the e/a burning on the ground. During the chase the drome lights had come on but they doused when the e/a was shot down..continued patrol until 02.35 ...crossed out between Ostend and Nieuport at 03.14 with searchlights and light flak active... landed at base 03.58 hours.

Late 1943: F/Sgt F Cassidy (Pilot) & F/Sgt CW Stickley (Nav)

Summer 1943: Mosquito MkII UP-A at Castle Camps

Summer 1943: 605 Commanding Officer W/Cdr Charles Tomalin A.F.C. on the steps of the crew ladder about to climb into Mosquito MkII UP-L

On the night 17th/18th Aug.1943 S/Ldr Mack and F/Sgt Harrison (later W/O and D.F.C.,) set off in a Mosquito to patrol and bomb Jagel aerodrome. During their patrol the aircraft was hit in the starboard wing by what was later found to be a cable projectile. The cable removed three feet of the wing and all but one foot of the aileron but was safely flown back to base and landed O.K. after the 430 mile trip home. The photos show clearly how the wing and aileron were severed.

June 1943: F/O Peter Wood & F/O Ray Smart at Castle Camps

> Bently Priory,
> Stanmore,
> Middlesex.
>
> 23rd.September 1943.
>
> Dear Group Captain,
>
> As I have just been posted to Fighter Command and the Squadron is being taken over by W/Cmd Hoare, I thought I would write to give you a short summary of the Squadron's achievements since it's re-formation, and to suggest that if you are over in the neighborhood a visit from you would be very much appreciated by everybody in the Squadron.
>
> The Squadron moved to Castle Camps from Ford on March 15th, but before the move three enemy aircraft had been destroyed and numerous ground targets had been attacked and damaged.
>
> On arrival at Castle Camps, there was a certain amount of depression due to the bleakness of the surroundings, in a very short time, however, the Squadron settled down to a profitable period despite the lack of activity on the part of the Hun.
>
> Since the re-formation of the Squadron, the successes have been as follows.
> ENEMY AIRCRAFT:- 20 destroyed, 3 probably destroyed, 9 damaged.
>
> LOCOMOTIVES; 5 destroyed, 79 damaged.
>
> AMMUNITION TRAINS: 2 destroyed.
>
> BARGES:- 15 damaged.
>
> TUGS:- 2 damaged.
>
> Our losses during this period were eight aircraft and crews, two of which were not due to enemy action.
> The Squadron's score since the beginning of the war as far as aircraft is concerned is, therefore,
> 90 destroyed, 22 probably destroyed, 49 damaged.
>
> The first day "Ranger" done by the Squadron was an outstanding success. F/Lt. Blomley and F/O Burrell planned a trip to Denmark but before they got there they knocked down two JU 88's and had to return due to lack of ammunition.
>
> I do hope you will be able to pay us a visit, especially as I am sure the new C.O. is very anxious to discuss the Squadron with you.
>
> Yours sincerely,

> B.R.O'B.H/DO.
>
> 605 Squadron,
> R.A.F.Station,
> Castle Camps,
> Cambs.
>
> 1st October 1943
>
> Dear Group Captain,
>
> I think Tomalin told you that he was leaving and I was taking over 605 and how glad I should be if you could come down and see the Squadron in the near future. There is a possibility of our moving quite soon to a more suitable base, so it would be advisable to drop a line or telephone beforehand.
>
> I think I am exceedingly lucky to have command of 605 and a better Squadron it would be hard to find and very soon I hope we shall be celebrating the destruction of our hundredth Hun. I don't know if you have any ideas as to what form the celebration should take, but I thought that a party for all ranks here as well as a sweepstake, the prize money to be divided between the air crew and ground crew who shoot down the 100th Hun and the winner of the ticket.
>
> Or perhaps you would like a more lasting memorial of this notable feat. Considering the time the Squadron was disbanded and non-operational it is a notable feat. I would be very grateful for any suggestions or help that you would like to give.
>
> Our score is now 96 and at the rate we are going we should reach the century within a month and this on Intruder work mostly over Germany - I think you will agree calls for some recognition for the whole Squadron who are all putting up a splendid show.
>
> Yours sincerely,
> B.R.o'B Hoare.
>
> Group Captain Lord Willoughby De Broke, M.C., A.F.C.,
> Air Ministry, King Charles Street,
> London, S.W.1.

Correspondence from W/Cdrs Charles Tomalin and Sammy Hoare to G/Cpt Lord Willoughby de Broke who was always eager for news of his old unit.

Flight Officer B.F.Miller (U.S.A.) with his navigator F/O J.C.Winlaw (R.C.A.F.).

This crew was posted to 605 on the 28th. Oct. '43 and operated with 'B' Flight. Both became very popular and during their tour they destroyed one E/A, damaged three and destroyed a 'Diver'. 'Bud's' rank, Flight Officer has no real equivalent in the R.A.F., - it being a sort of commissioned Warrant Officer, and he was granted this rank when he transferred to the U.S.A.A.F. from the R.A.F. where he had been intending to join one of the 'Eagle Squadrons'.

Not only were they a very useful operational crew, but the Squadron blessed them for the good they did on the welfare side. Winnie's mother in Canada used to periodically send over parcels of woollen goods, pullovers, socks, etc., which had been knitted by her friends and these were distributed amongst the airmen. Then Bud used to go 'scrounging' from the American Army Welfare Center and produced such things as a radio, footballs, and the inevitable baseball bats and balls which came in very useful. In fact, at Coxyde in the summer of '45 the Squadron was able to field quite a good 'soft ball' team to play our Canadian partners on the Wing, 418 Squadron, who previously had been our rivals when both Squadrons were the home-based Intruders of Fighter Command.

Brussels/Melsbroek was the happy hunting ground for Bud and he got his one destroyed and two of the damaged there. Quite a change from his first visit there on the 11/12th Nov. '43 doing an Operational training trip. Then for the whole hour of his patrol, 'Bud' plodded round and round the drome dodging the flak and came back wondering whether intruding was quite the thing, and as attractive as he had thought. He soon learned, however, and later was to go in and beat up the drome without getting hit.

In fact it wasn't at Melsbroek but at Ober/Olm in Germany that his aircraft was badly hit after an attack on the drome. Then he returned with the tail cone and light shot off, 20 holes in the tailplane and five in the fuselage, but the Hun aircraft he had attacked was in far worse shape.

Associated Press Photo shows:- Pilot Officer M.G. McManus, D.F.M., of S. Shields (Left) who has been on 46 sorties, and Pilot Officer Raymond Jones, D.F.C., who has been on 53 sorties.

Summer 1943: Sgt Sidney Didsbury (Nav) and F/O Ken Dacre (Pilot) at Castle Camps

```
3                    F/O Dacre.                        60
O.C.P.   GPK NR HFC 245/21 NOTWT                    21 JUN 1943
PASS 1ST ADD

TO FLYING OFFICER DACRE. SERGEANT DIDSBURY 605 SQDN CASTLE CAMPS (R)
NO 11 GROUP
FROM AxxxxxXxxxx AOC-IN-C HQ FIGHTER COMMAND
C78 21 JUNE HEARTIES CONGRATULATIONS ON YOUR VERY SUCCESSFULL
  OPERATION ON THE NIGHT OV XXXX OF 19/20TH . WELL DONE LEIGH-
MALLORY = 212140B
EVG/VA++

GPK     R 202331B     DB VA+
```

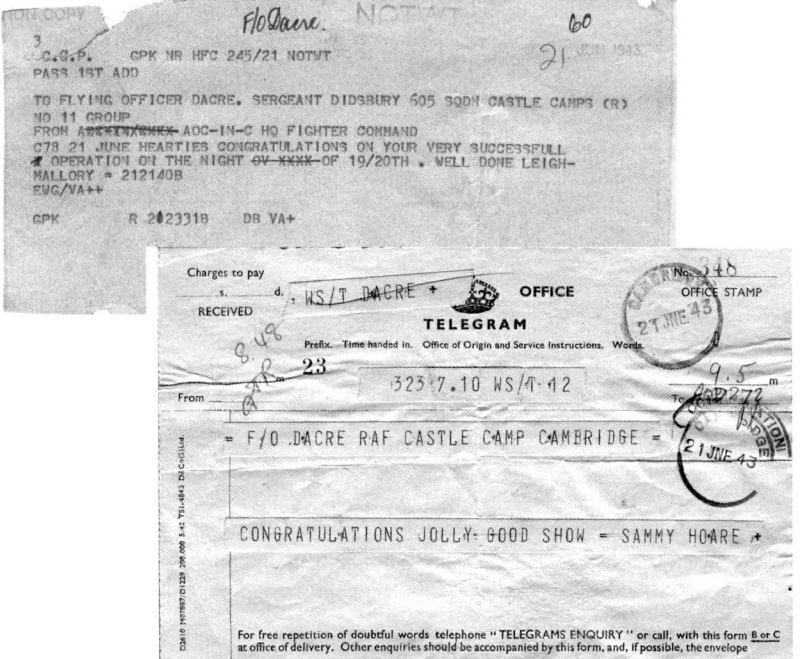

TELEGRAM — F/O DACRE RAF CASTLE CAMP CAMBRIDGE
= CONGRATULATIONS JOLLY GOOD SHOW = SAMMY HOARE +

---

605 SQUADRON.   INTELLIGENCE FORM "F" AND PERSONAL COMBAT REPORT.   SECRET.   E.15.

From: R.A.F. Station, Castle Camps, Cambs.   Serial No. 9.

To: Headquarters Fighter Command (2 copies)., HQ No.11 Group., O.C. Castle Camps., S.I.O., I.O. 605 Sqdn (6 copies) and File.

STATISTICAL.
Date;   (A) 19th/20th June 1943.
Unit;   (B) 605 (County of Warwick) Squadron. A.A.F.
Type and mark of our aircraft;   (C) Mosquito II.
Time attack was delivered;   (D) 0125 and 0208 hours.
Place of attack and/or target;   (E) Compiegne/Margny & St. Dizier/Robinson.
Weather;   (F) Vis. very good, some valley mist. No cloud.
Our casualties - aircraft;   (G) Nil.
    "   - personnel;   (H) Nil.
Enemy casualties, in air combat;   (J) 1 Do 217 Destroyed, 1 Me 110 Destroyed.
    "   , ground or sea target;   (K) 1 Locomotive destroyed. (Cat A).
                                             1 Locomotive Cat.B., 1 Locomotive Cat.C.

Pilot: F/O Dacre.   Observer: Sgt. Didsbury.

One Mosquito II, UP/O, took off from Castle Camps at 0023 hours for Intruder patrol to St. Dizier, and after crossing the Channel at 500 feet made landfall at Ault at 0104 hours, 2000 feet. The Pilot's report continues:-

"At about 0121 hours we arrived at Compiegne/Margny which was lit up with red perimeter lights and a single flarepath of eight white lights, running N - S which doused as we went by, but came on again after we had passed. About one minute later while at 1500 feet we sighted a Do.217 approaching head-on with a white light under its tail, and it passed above us on the port side at about 1800 ft. I turned sharply to port and chased at full throttle catching up to about 300 yards and giving a short burst of 1/2 second, but did not observe any results. The E/A started to turn to port and descend and as it was passing over the aerodrome I opened fire again with one ring deflection, the aerodrome defences opening up at the same time with light tracer. I thereupon closed in and gave a third short burst at which the port engine caught fire, and the E/A started to descend in a long glide, flames spreading to the fuselage and starboard engine. After a glide of three to four miles the E/A finally crashed 4 miles "." of the aerodrome, bursting into flames. I made one run over the wreckage using my cine-camera and we resumed course at 0126 hrs for St. Dizier, which we reached at 0205 hrs. After we had completed one half circuit, my observer sighted a red airborne light going down the middle of the Lorenz at the E end of the E/W runway at 500 feet. I made a diving turn to the left and opened fire at 0208 hrs (On the E/A's port side from 100 yds, the E/A then being at 500 ft.), just as the E/A switched on its landing light. The E/A caught fire in the cockpit and we were then able to identify it as an Me 110. I turned sharply right to avoid going over the centre of the aerodrome and my observer saw the E/A crash about 1/2 mile to the E of the aerodrome where it burned on the ground, ammunition being seen exploding in all directions. All the aerodrome lighting was doused, but came on again shortly afterwards, this time with the N/S flarepath instead of as before. We continued our patrol until 0234 hrs when we set course for home. When passing Vitry le Francois at 0237 hrs we found and attacked a train. The firebox of the locomotive was seen to be disembowelled and spread itself over the railway track and is claimed destroyed. We saw a second train in the vicinity but did not attack. A third train was sighted and attacked at Vitry-la-ville at 0252 hrs and we saw strikes on the engine tender and the train came to a halt in a cutting (Cat.C) and we attacked a fourth at 0253 hrs just N. of Chalons-sur-Marne, three times observing strikes on the engine, tender and first coach, the train coming to a halt (Cat.B)".

The intruder then set course for base, 0255 hrs, and arriving at Ault at 0330 hrs crossed out over the Channel at 1500 ft. and landed at base at 0405 hours.
NOTE: It is presumed that, from the direction in which the Me 110 at St. Dizier was attempting to land, i.e. E/W that the runway is now complete.

Sgd. R.C.Treweeks.   Sgd. K.F.Dacre.
Flying Officer. Intelligence.   Flying Officer. "B" Flight.
605 (A) Squadron.   605 (A) Squadron.
R.A.F. Station. Castle Camps.   R.A.F. Station. Castle Camps.

FLYING OFFICER K.F.DACRE, D.F.C., and SERGEANT S.R.DIDSBURY, D.F.M.

On the 5th. April 1943, Pilot Officer K.F.Dacre and his observer Sgt. S.R.Didsbury were posted to 605. A few months later they were the Sqdn's most successful crew and by September they had destroyed 4 E/A, probably destroyed a 5th and damaged another. Both displayed exceptional skill and enthusiasm for Ops and they were both an inspiration to all members of the Squadron. In September 1943, they were awarded the D.F.C. and D.F.M. respectively but a few nights earlier tragically did not return from an Intruder sortie to Ardorf.

"Dicer", as Ken Dacre was generally called, usually wore a scarf on trips and this scarf, bearing the name "L.White" or similar initials, was the clue that eventually led to the discovery that their bodies (Dacre's and Didsbury's) were buried in the New Cemetery, Oldenburg, Div.1, Sect III, Row X. Photo's show the row of graves but unfortunately at the time they were taken the cross was being re-painted. Examination of the cemetery records showed that they had been interred as "unknown" and it is hoped that this state of affairs will be remedied. The man in charge at the cemetery stated that they had been killed when the Mosquito hit some high tension cables, but his memory may not be correct.

Three of their combat reports are given in full here as examples of their magnificent operational spirit - rarely did they return without having found some target for their guns and on one trip alone they attacked 8 trains.
A truly magnificent crew.

CURRENT TOPICS
Trophy For R.A.F.
Memorial Gift By Air Commodore and Mrs. Dacre : Son's Keenness Set An Example

A TROPHY, which is to be awarded annually to the regular squadron of Fighter Command showing the greatest proficiency in weapons training, has been presented to the

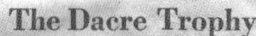

Royal Air Force by Air Commodore G. B. Dacre, C.B.E., D.S.O., D.L., R.A.F. (ret.), and Mrs. Dacre, J.P. It is in memory of their son, Flying Officer Kenneth Fraser Dacre, D.F.C., who was killed in action over Germany in 1943.

The Dacre trophy, which is of bronze mounted on a marble base, is in the form of three classical archers. The artist is Mr. A. E. Sean Crampton, G.M., M.C. It will be awarded to the Fighter Command squadron achieving the best results during the annual attendance at armament practice camp, when squadrons will be assessed on their previous 12 months' weapon training effort. Emphasis will be placed on live air-to-air-firing and all squadron pilots must compete.

Flying Officer Dacre, who was 21 at the time of his death, entered the R.A.F. in 1940 and in 1943 joined No. 605 (County of Warwick) Squadron, which was then engaged on night intruder operations. After 24 operational sorties, during which he destroyed three enemy aircraft (two of them in one night), one locomotive and damaged 13 more locomotives, he was killed while flying over North-Western Germany in September 1943. When Flying Officer Dacre's D.F.C. award was announced in October, 1943, he was described as "a most determined pilot, whose keenness has set a highly commendable example."

NOTABLE SERVICE

Air Commodore Dacre learned to fly in 1911 (his pilot's certificate is No. 162) and served in the Royal Naval Air Service in the First World War, winning the D.S.O. for flying operations in the Dardenelles. In September, 1939, he went to France as Air Officer in charge of Administration, Advanced Air Striking Force, and after the evacuation, was reappointed to Command R.A.F. Station, Halton. On his retirement from the service, in 1944, he became Commandant of St. Dunstan's. In 1948 he was made Sussex County President of the British Legion. He is vice-chairman of the Sussex Territorial and Auxiliary Forces Association and a Deputy Lieutenant of Sussex.

Mrs. Dacre served throughout the war in the W.A.A.F., attaining the rank of Group Officer.

F/Sgt. S. Weston with two of his pilots.
On the left he is with F/Sgt W. Irving (later W/O) who successfully completed two tours of Ops with 605. The photo on right shows F/Sgt Weston with F/Sgt H.J. Collins. (later W/O). Irving first joined the Squadron in Nov. '42 and completed his first tour in Jan. '44. He was then posted to O.T.U. as an instructor and returned to the Squadron in Aug. '44. He remained until after VE Day and was posted in June '45.
H.J. Collins joined 605 in July '42 and by March '43 had completed 7 sorties. He was then posted to join 23 Sqdn who were then intruding from Malta and did 7 ops with them only to return to 605 in June '43 with whom he did a further 20 trips. He then went to O.T.U. as an instructor from Feb.'44 to Aug.'44 when he rejoined 605 and remained with us till he was unfortunately killed in a flying accident at Croydon in an Oxford on 3rd Aug. '45.
The following is extracted from a personal combat report following a sortie on the night of 27/28th.Sept.'43 when Collins was a Sgt. and was flying with Sgt. D.A.W.Norton:-
".......took off Castle Camps 2049 hrs......to patrol dromes in Vechta area.....then coast crossed at Egmond at 2134.........patrolled Hesepe 2207.......then Lembruch at 2212 .....then to Diepholz which was alight at 2219hrs....remained patrolling aerodromes round the Dummer Zee until at 2304 hrs an e/a was seen with nav. lights on....we chased this e/a to Diepholz and followed him down the V/L..... closing so fast I only had time to fire a 1 sec burst of cannon at his tail at 400 feet from 200 yards range closing to 50 yards before overshooting as he touched down, and we saw no results.....at 2308 hrs we sighted a second e/a..attempted a beam attack as he touched down from 700 feet range 500 yards..... saw strikes on runway ahead of him and two of the flare path lights went out...2310 hrs we sighted a third e/a going in to land at Diepholz....gave chase and he decided to go to Vechta...we chased him there...nearing Vechta I called up F/Sgt Irving who was patrolling the area with us, to say that I was about to make an attack over his aerodrome. He replied that he was going to attack the same e/a, warning me in words that cast a reflection on my parentage to keep away, but in the excitement of the moment neither my observer nor I heard him, though others in different areas did. Not receiving any reply to his message he broke away, and at 2311 hrs, 250 yards range, from 100 feet I gave a 1 or 2 second burst of cannon only....saw strikes on starboard engine and 10 secs later he crashed into a wood N. of the drome.....made a run over and took a photograph and then saw another e/a coming in to land E - W......we attacked at 500 feet at 2315 hrs from dead astern at 150 yards range giving a 1 - 2 sec burst of cannon only and the e/a went straight in. Both these attacks and their results were witnessed by F/Sgt Irving, much to his annoyance.....left target area at 2323 hrs... landed base at 0055 hrs."

Associated Press Photo shows:- Sgt. Ray Phillips,(left) of Chiswick, who is credited with 13 sorties and Flying Officer Jack Reid, of Glasgow, who has been on 39 sorties.

The above two photographs were taken by the Press at Bradwell Bay, Essex, and written up as above. This was early in 1944. Tragically, F/O J. Reid and P/O R.E. Phillips were killed when the Mosquito they were flying on an N.F.T.(Night Flying Test) on the 26th. June 1944 appeared to blow up over Margate and crashed in flames. They only had to complete another sortie before going on a 'rest' as F/O Reid had almost completed his second tour of Ops and P/O Phillips his first. McManus and Jones successfully completed their 2nd. tour of Operations with 605 Squadron. Their first tour was with 23 Squadron, the Mosquito Intruder Squadron which operated with much success from Malta and later, Sicily.

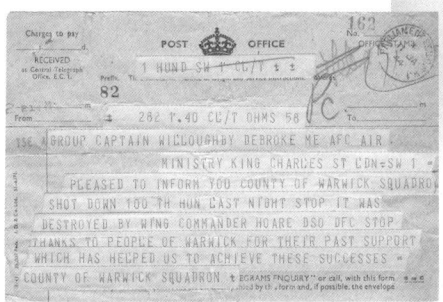

Jan 1944: On the night of 11th Jan 1944, W/Cdr Sammy Hoare and F/O Bob Muir shot down 605's 100th enemy aircraft.

W/Cdr. B.R.O'B.Hoare. D.S.O and Bar, D.F.C. and Bar. Mention in Despatches was Officer Commanding from the 25th. Sept. 1943 to 10th. April 1944 during which period the Squadron destroyed 33 enemy aircraft, probably destroyed 2 and damaged 35. He was awarded a Bar to his D.S.O. in March 1944 for "Magnificent leadership" and also mentioned in despatches in Jan. 1944. During this month he shot down what was at that time thought to be the Squadron's 100th. enemy aircraft destroyed - a Ju. 188 which was trying to land at Chievres.

F/Lt. A.D. Wagner, D.F.C., and F/O E.T. Orringe, with their "War-Wagon", "J" for Johnnie.

W/Cdr. R.A. Mitchell, D.F.C., and Bar with navigator, F/Lt. S.H. Hatsell, D.F.C.,

The greatest tragedy to the members of 605 was the loss of their Nav. Officer with the C.O. they worshipped on the 17th. March 1945, the first night the Squadron operated from Coxyde, Belgium.

'Mitch' and Stan were first posted to the Squadron in Nov.'43 as S/Ldr. (Super-numery) and P/O respectively. Together they successfully operated until April '44, and in that time collected 3½ destroyed and 4 damaged. This was 'Mitch's' third tour of Ops and already he had a few Huns behind him. In Feb. '44 he became 'A' Flight Commander and was promoted to Wing Commander on posting to the Intruder O.T.U, as Chief Instructor on the 11th. April '44. They created a night record for Intruders when they destroyed three and damaged three in one night's sortie on the 5th/6th. April '44.

Stan carried on operating and crewed up with F/O E.L. Williams, D.F.C., and together they destroyed three, probably destroyed one and damaged four more Huns before Stan was posted on 14th. July '44. W/Cdr. Mitchell had meanwhile been awarded a Bar to his D.F.C., and on the 28th. July '44, Stan was awarded the D.F.C..

On the 17th. Sept. '44, Mitch returned to 605, this time to command it and three days later Stan rolled up to navigate him. Encouraging the Daylight Rangers, Mitch had the Squadron topping Fighter Command's monthly score sheet in October when 605 destroyed 23, probably destroyed 2 and damaged 13 !! Mitch and Stan collected 3 destroyed themselves in one daylight sortie. Stan was then Nav. Officer and an Acting Fl/Lt.

In November '44, the Squadron left Fighter Command and joined No.2 Group, 2nd. T.A.F. on the 21st. and during the next 6 weeks were non-operational. In this trying time when everyone was considerably fed up with the enforced inactivity and training, Mitch held the Squadron together as no-one else could have done. At last, in Dec.'44, 605 became operational again and Mitch and Stan were the first to take off of the eleven crews that operated that night (the 31st).

Happy again, 605 carried on in fair weather and foul, going from strength to strength under Mitch in their new role - night interdiction. Then on the night of the 17th/18th. March '45 came tragedy - Mitch and Stan failed to return and nothing has been heard of them since. 605 carried on and followed the example they set.

F/O 'Pip' Orringe arrived on the Squadron in July 1943 with S/Ldr. Taylor.A.F.C. as his pilot. He was soon named 'Beauvais' Orringe, as a few of his earlier trips took him to this enemy occupied airfield and for a long while rumour had it that he could not find the drome for his pilot to patrol. However this may possibly have been the result of a very sweeping and misguided statement he once was heard to make to the Squadron Navigation Officer......"You can't teach me anything about map-reading"!!. Whatever the truth he later crewed up with F/Lt. A.D. Wagner, D.F.C., in October 1943, when 'Wag' joined the Squadron with some 118 sorties to his credit, and 3 Hun E/A destroyed plus two Jap. Zero's destroyed. By the time they were posted on the 1st. May 1944, together they had destroyed a further 6 enemy aircraft, probably destroyed 1, and damaged 4. 'Wag' was awarded a Bar to his D.F.C., and 'Pip' received a D.F.C.. Tragically they continued operations, with F.I.U., and then Wag went to 501 Squadron, were flying Tempests at night he reaped havoc against the flying bombs before being killed returning to base in duff weather one night.

This crew's magnificent determination and offensive spirit are illustrated by the combat report dated the 5/6th. March 1944, which is given here

25/1/44: Scotish Paring of P/O Eric Cosby & F/Sgt Robertson, Note the Lion Rampant on their crew door.

"Never Sleep" Squadron Gets Its 100th Hun

ONE of the most successful home-based R.A.F. intruder squadrons, the No. 605 (County of Warwick) Auxiliary Air Force squadron, which has for its motto "I Never Sleep," celebrated the destruction of its 100th victim with a dinner party at the Dorchester Hotel, London.

Twenty-six pre-war members of the squadron were the hosts and the guests were thirty members of the present squadron.

Presiding over this group of past and present fighters was the Honorary Air Commodore, Sir Lindsay Everard, M.P., who presented the members with a silver "Mosquito" bearing the identical marks of the machine flown by Wing Commander B. R. O. B. Hoare when he completed the squadron's century of victims.

Mobilised in 1939, with 29 pilots, the squadron helped to defend Scotland and North Sea shipping, battled at Dunkirk and won about half its victories in the Battle of Britain.

Ordered abroad in 1941 it was chosen to defend the Dutch East Indies, where the members became prisoners of the Japanese.

Reformed in 1942 and equipped with Boston fighter bombers the squadron became night intruders. Mosquitos replaced Bostons and the "Never Sleeps" prowled over enemy territory steadily building up their fine record. At the dinner many old members saw the squadron's new badge—the Warwickshire bear and ragged staff in the standard R.A.F. surround—and recalled how the motto, "Nunquam Dormio," came to be adopted.

In its early days the squadron held annual camps at Manston in Kent. Returning to camp in the early hours some convivial members found an evening newspaper poster which read "Sleep is just a waste of time."

The poster was duly framed and hung for many years in the mess at Castle Bromwich. The motto originated from these words. It has become singularly apt.

This squadron of night fighters has gained 1 D.S.O., 17 D.F.C.'s 1 bar to D.F.C, 2 D.F.M.'s, 3 A.F.C.'s and 7 mentions in despatches

The present total of kills credited to the squadron is 127.

BELFAST TELEGRAPH.
25 APR 1944.

April 1944: F/O Leo Williams D.F.C. admires the silver Mosquito that was presented to W/Cdr Sammy Hoare D.S.O. D.F.C. by 605 Honorary Air Commodore Sir Lindsay Everard M.P. (far right). Also pictured (2nd right) is 605's first CO, G/Cpt J.A.C. Wright.

W/Cdr Sammy Hoare D.S.O. D.F.C. and S/Ldr Knowles D.F.C & Bar

April 1944: A dinner was held to commorate 605's 100th enemy aircraft destroyed. A number of pre-war officers were invited. L-R: 605 Honorary Air Commodore Sir Lindsay Everard M.P., W/Cdr Cyril Longsdon, G/Cpt Lord Willoughby de Broke M.C. A.F.C. and G/Cpt Gerry Edge D.F.C.

June 1944: LACW Lynn Bagge, F/O Jock Reid D.F.M. & LACW Cherry Pring. Lynn & Cherry were posted to 605 as WAAF MT Drivers. Jock was killed a few days after this photo was taken.

"A" Flight at Manston, July 1944.
Front row, L. to R., P/O C.L. Burrage (missing Oct'44), F/O R. Burrows, F/O G. Phillips (missing Feb'45), F/O L.J. Gibson (Intell), F/S F.W. Samwell, F/S J.H. Little, Sgt. T. Caulfield (missing Feb'45-P.O.W.), F/S C.R. Couchman, W/O J.W. Tredwen (later 'Mentioned'), F/O S.F. Melloy, F/O G.H. Allen, W/O T. Harris (missing Aug'44-P.O.W.), F/O C.G. Gibson (missing Jan'45). R.A.A.F.
2nd. row;-F/L B.G. Bensted (missing Oct'44), F/L A.V. Rix D.F.M., F/L E.L. Jones (missing Feb'45) F/L R.C. Walton (N.Z.), F/L J.G. Musgrave, F/L J. Rhodes, S/L I.F. McCall (missing Feb '45-P.O.W.-laterD.F.C.), F/L J.I. Pengelly (later D.F.C.), F/L A.M. Michie (later 'Mentioned'), F/L P.S. Compton, F/L P.F. Middleton, F/O R.O. Brigden (missing Aug'44-), F/O G.M. Lumsden (missing Jan'45) R.A.A.F.
3rd. row; -L/A/C's Phillips, McGowan, Norton. Cpls Smart, Peffers, Staniland, Sgt. Phillips, F/S Freeman-Pannett, Sgt. Tryner, Cpls Chesterneuf, Murray. L/A/C's Becket, Biltcliffe, James, and Cpl Kemp.
Back row;-L/A/C's Wem, Strange, Fifield, Webb, Chamberlain, Mills, Orme, Bullman, Sell, Evans, Twells, Mullins and Burchell.

6/6/1944 'D-Day': 605 were in action early in the morning of 'D-Day', in support of the allied airborne landings in Northern France. Our brief included attacking enemy searchlight and ack-ack positions prior to the mass Allied parachute drops early in the morning. 605 put up a total of 18 aircraft, most of which left Manston just before midnight. F/O Roy Lelong and F/Sgt McLaren were sent to the Evreux and St Andre areas, crossing the French coast at 0020 hrs. On arrival they found both airfields to be inactive. At 0130 hrs the airfield at St Andre lit up and moments later as Roy was just about to make a bomb attack the lights were extinguished. Despite this he made another run and dropped two 500lb and two 250lb bombs on the aerodrome. Minutes later it was the turn of Evreux to light up and Roy obtained a visual on an aircraft at 1000 feet silhouetted against the clouds, and with the help of the moon he recognised it as an Me.410. Lelong closed in to position himself just underneath the enemy aircraft. He then throttled back and pulled up to dead astern and at a range of 150 yards opened fire with a 1 1/2 second burst at a height of 1000 feet. Strikes were seen around the cockpit area and the aircraft then burst into flames, in the light of which it was without doubt confirmed as an Me.410. It then lost height slowly in a spiral dive and finally crashed about 7 miles south-east of Evreux airfield. The attack was timed at 0148 and was later confirmed as being the first enemy aircraft destroyed by any unit on the morning of D-Day.

Apr 43: Some of 'B' Flight relaxing at Castle Camps:
Back row: 1st right – P/O J.K. Sutcliffe
Middle row: F/O Arthur Woods (with pipe)
Front row: 3rd left - F/Lt Arthur Mack (later D.F.C.), 4th left - Sgt Robert Brown (killed 23/4/1943), 1st right - F/O Peter D.J. Wood (later D.F.C.)

22/12/43: Cockpit of Mk.VI Mosquito HJ785 UP-T

W/Cdr N.J.Starr, D.F.C., and P/O J.Irvine inspecting the tail of the Mosquito in which they destroyed an enemy aircraft on the night of the 17th/18th July 1944. P/O Irvine completed two tours of operations with the Squadron and was awarded the D.F.C. in August 1944. Following is extracted from the combat report:-"Airborne at 2348hours - arrived in Schwabsiche-Hall area at 0135 - e/a seen at 3000ft burning navigation lights - it was attacked from very short range 20-50 yds still overtaking at 6000 feet with a 1/3rd sec. burst of cannon only - a brilliant explosion occurred which completely blinded W/Cdr Starr and the aircraft was seemingly struck by several pieces of the e/a. W/Cdr Starr estimates he was completely blind for three minutes during which time P/O Irvine gave directions to enable the aircraft to be flown very erratically - the rudder was found to be jammed but the engines appeared to be functioning correctly with slight vibrations. Landed at base at 0350 hrs." On inspection of the aircraft in daylight it was found that all the paint on the fuselage, tailplane, and mainplane inboard of the engines had been burnt away, and 1/3rd of the rudder surface was missing, 1 blade of the port prop was bent forward and the whole perspex hood was black with oil. There was a 6 inch hole in the port side of the nose and a piece of Hun landing wheel tyre was lodged just behind the instrument panel and bits of wood scattered over the cockpit.

'B' Flight at Manston after 'D' Day, June 1944.
'D' Day found the aircrew wearing artillery. From left to right we see;- Sgt. J.A.McLaren (later P/O and D.F.C.,), F/O B.J.Duncan, P/O A.J.Davey, F/O A.T.Linn (later D.F.C.,), W/O W.Harrison (later D.F.C.,), S/Ldr. K.M.Carver (later D.F.C.,), F/O R.E.Leleng (N.Z. and later D.F.C.,), F/Sgt. W.J.Robertson, F/O S.H.Hatsell (later D.F.C.,), F/Lt. G.C. Wright. A.F.C., Flight Officer B.F.Miller (U.S.A.A.C.), P/O J.C.Winlaw (R.C.A.F.), F/Lt. P.J.Garner, Sgt L.W.Woodard (later D.F.M.,).

'A' Flight with Ground Crew at Bradwell Bay in March 1944.

Front row, left to right:- L/A/C's Mills, Evans, Howard, Norman, Colley, Moore, Sibley.
Second row, left to right:- F/O R.C.Walton, F/O R.G.Collins, F/O S.H.Hatsell (later D.F.C.,), F/O J.G.Musgrave, F/O G.A.Holland, F/Lt. A.D.Wagner D.F.C.,(later and Bar), S/Ldr. J.F.Evans, S/Ldr. R.A.Mitchell D.F.C.,(and Bar, later), F/Lt. T.L.M. Woods, F/Lt. J.R.Beckett, F/O E.T.Orringe (later D.F.C.,), F/Lt. J. Rhodes, F/O P.D.Topping, F/O K.H.Ray, F/O R.H.Wilkinson.
Third row, left to right:- Cpl Green, L/A/C Royston, Sgt. F.Pritchard, Sgt. C.R.Couchman, Sgt. J.H.Litile, F/Sgt. D.A.W.Norton, Sgt. F.Cassidy, Sgt. 'Slash' Phillips, F/Sgt. Freeman-Pannett, Sgt. Grimes, F/Sgt. C.W.Stickley, F/Sgt. H.V.Morrison, F/Sgt. F.Stirling, F/Sgt. F.W.Samwell, Sgt. R.A.Bond, Cpl. Gregory, L/A/C Homer.
Back row, left to right:- Cpl. Baker, ? , L/A/C Craig, A/C's Hodgson, Nicholl, Jones, Cpl. Page, A/C's Lawrence, Newstead, Evans, Townley, Loxley, Baxter, Cpl. Fox, A/C's Richards, Samson, Chamberlain, Dinnecombe, Wright, Joslin, Cpl. Cowell.

Three 'Aces' together:- 'Mitch' with F/Lt Alan Wagner and W/Cdr. 'Sammy' Hoare, photographed in the Ops Room at Bradwell Bay

F/O A.T.Linn. D.F.C.,
Posted from O.T.U. to 605 Sqdn on 19th Aug 1942 as a Sgt, Arture Linn was promoted Flight Sgt and in August 1943 he was commissioned as a Pilot Officer. His enthusiasm brought success on this tour and he destroyed a Do 217 and a Me 210 with his navigator F/O May. On one occasion in daylight when he was attacking some Ju 52's which were escorted by Fw 190's he narrowly escaped being shot down himself and returned with his elevator holed by cannon fire from a 190. In Nov 1943 he completed his first tour and for 6 months helped to train pilots at an O.T.U. where he gave dual instruction on Mosquito's. On the 2nd June 1944 he returned to 605 for another tour and this time his navigator was W/O W.Harrison also returning to the Squadron after 6 months 'rest'. Again followed a very successful tour during which time they attacked flying bombs and the enemy's communications and transport until March 1945 when their tour expired. By this time F/O Linn had completed some 85 sorties mainly by night and his experiences ranged from Intruder patrols to T.A.F. patrols with Bomber Support patrols, Daylight Rangers, and Anti-Diver patrols thrown in for full measure. During one of the latter he pressed home his attack to such close range,that when the flying bomb exploded as his shells hit same,he had to fly through the debris and return with a much damaged aircraft and one engine completely out of action. During his last sortie when making a third determined attack to completely destroy a train,light flak from the train hit the Mosquito and one of the shells entering the cockpit removed the engine petrol cut-out controls and another pierced W/O Harrison's maps. Neither were injured at all. During this tour they destroyed 2 flying bombs and damaged a Fw 190 apart from numerous Hun transport which they successfully attacked. In June 1945 both Linn and Harrison were awarded the D.F.C.'s they so well deserved and in this month F/O Linn again returned to 605 Squadron to start his 3rd tour,though by then the war in Europe was over.
F/O Linn came over from Uruguay to join the R.A.F.

W/Cdr. N.J.Starr. D.F.C., and Bar. Officer Commanding from 10th. April 1944 to 20th. Sept. 1944. Awarded Bar to D.F.C., in Nov.1944. Unfortunately W/Cdr. Starr was later shot down by the Dunkirk defences when non-operationally flying between the Continent and England.

F/O R.C.Muir, on the far right in the photo was one of the star navigators of 605. Joining the Squadron shortly after it reformed as a Pilot Officer in '42, he stayed operational until he was posted in April 1944. During this period he operated over 50 times and shared as navigator in destroying two E/A, probably destroying a third and damaging three. He flew with W/Cdr Tomalin, D.F.C., A.F.C., and with W/Cdr. Hoare, D.S.O., D.F.C. regularly and on occasions with S/Ldr. Heath, A.F.C. and Bar. His keenness to operate was demonstrated on one memorable occasion when leaving the Ops room at Bradwell Bay to fly with S/Ldr. Heath and making his way out to the aircraft in the darkness he fell into some water. He was completely soaked - so were his maps and helmet etc., but nevertheless though it was in the winter and very cold, he clambered into the aircraft and did not say a word until the pilot had to cancel his trip as he could not get a word out of the inter-com and R/T owing to the deafening whistle caused by Bob's wet helmet. Needless to say this became the subject of numerous jokes in the next few weeks, and it took some time for Bob to live it down. In April '44, he was awarded a very well-earned D.F.C.,

This is the only photograph available which shows S/Ldr. M.Negus,D.F.C., and his navigator, F/O A.F.Gapper who did not return from a sortie on the night of the 6/7th April '44. They were posted in on the 28th. Oct. '43, and F/Lt Negus had already some 72 Coastal Command Ops behind him. From one of these, in 1940, he had brought a badly damaged Hudson safely home although himself wounded and his first pilot seriously so. All maps and navigational aids had been blown out of the aircraft. With this background he soon made a name for himself and before he went missing with his navigator they had destroyed three E/A and damaged two more. In February 1944, Negus was appointed 'B' Flight Commander and succeeded S/Ldr. D.H.Blomeley, D.F.C., In April '44 on a sortie to Strasbourg and Lake Constance this crew failed to return and from information received shortly afterwards it is believed that they crashed into the Lake, but the cause is unknown. Later in the month it was learned that S/Ldr. Negus had been awarded the D.F.C.,

A group of the Squadron aircrew taken in the Ops Room at Bradwell Bay in 1944.

Back row, left to right:- F/Lt. A.D.Wagner, D.F.C., and Bar; F/Lt. W.A.Bird, D.F.C.,; F/Lt. L.H.Hodder, D.F.C.,; F/O R.C.Southcott, Intelligence Officer.
Front row, left to right:- F/O F.E.Hogg (NZ) D.F.C., and Bar; F/O E.T.Orringe, D.F.C., F/O E.L.Williams, D.F.C., (Rhodesia); F/O A.F.Gapper; S/Ldr. M.Negus, D.F.C., F/O R.C.Muir, D.F.C.,

Bradwell Bay. March 1944. 605 Aircrew with the senior N.C.O's, ground crew.

Front row, left to right:- Sgt's Hanson, Phillips, Grimes, Williamson, ? (Inst. Sect.); F/Sgt's Freeman-Pannett, Cole, Lyddiatt and Sgt's Griffin, Tryner, Bartholomew, and F/Sgt Robertson.
Seated, second row, left to right:- F/Lt. G.C.Wright, A.F.C., F/Lt. A.D.Wagner, D.F.C. (and Bar, later), F/Lt. T.L.M.Woods, F/Lt. D.J.N.Rebbeck. (later M.B.E.,), F/Lt. K.M.Carver (later D.F.C.,), F/Lt. J.D.Thomas, S/Ldr. R.A.Mitchell. D.F.C., (and Bar, later), W/Cdr. B.R.O'B.Hoare. D.S.O., and Bar, D.F.C., and Bar, S/Ldr. M.Negus (later D.F.C.,), S/Ldr. J.F.Evans, F/Lt. W.A.Bird (later D.F.C.,), F/Lt. J.R.Beckett, F/Lt. A.C.Dunn. M.B.E., F/Lt. L.H.Hodder (later D.F.C.,).
Third row, left to right:- F/O R.S.Jones. D.F.C., F/O M.G.McManus. D.F.M., F/O F.D.Topping, F/O R.G.Collins, F/Lt. A.C.Woodley.D.F.C., F/Lt. J.Rhodes, F/O J.G.Musgrave, F/O R.C.Walton, F/Lt. G.F.Allison, F/O R.P.Bourne, F/O A.J.Gapper, F/Lt. G.J.Wright, F/O G.A.Holland, F/O R.H.Wilkinson, F/O S.H.Hatsell (later D.F.C.,), F/O E.T.Orringe (later D.F.C.,), F/O R.C.Muir (later D.F.C.,), F/O K.H.Ray,
Back row, left to right:- Sgt. F. Cassidy, Sgt. Brannigan, F/Sgt. C.W.Stickley, F/Sgt. F.W.Samwell, F/Sgt. D.A.W. Norton, F/Sgt. F. Stirling, Sgt. J.A.McLaren (later D.F.C.,), F/Lt. I.J.Cramond, F/O R.Birrell, Pt. Off. B.F.Miller, F/O J.C.Winlaw, F/O R.E.Lelong (later D.F.C.,), W/O A.H.Wettone, Sgt. F.Pritchard, Sgt. C.R.Couchman, F/Sgt. R.H.Sutcliffe, Sgt. J.H.Little, F/Sgt. Walker, Sgt. Rawlings.

SECRET.

From: No. 605 (County of Warwick) Squadron, R.A.F. Station, Manston.

To: Headquarters A.D.G.B. (2)., Headquarters No.11 Group (2)., Nos. 418 and 29 Sqdns., R.A.F. Hunsdon, No. 60 O.T.U. High Ercall., Intelligence, Manston, S.I.O., No. 605 Sqdn (8).

Serial No. 60/Jan. 38.

PERSONAL COMBAT REPORT.

STATISTICAL.

Date;   (A) 11th. October, 1944.
Unit;   (B) 605 (County of Warwick) Squadron.
Type and mark of aircraft; (C) Mosquito VI.
Time attack was delivered; (D) 1030 - 1035 hours.
Place of attack;   (E) PLESO A/F. (ii) ZAGREB A/F. High scattered cloud.
Weather;   (F) Excellent visibility. High scattered cloud.
Our casualties - aircraft; (G) Mosquito VI Cat. AC.
               - personnel;   (H) Nil.
Enemy casualties - in air combat; (J) Nil.
               - ground or sea targets; (K) (i) 1 Me 110 Destroyed.
                                          (ii) 2 Ju 87's Destroyed.

Pilot. W/Cdr. R.A.Mitchell D.F.C. and Bar.   Navigator. F/Lt. S.H.Mitcell D.F.C.

DAY RANGER - BUDAPEST AREA.

Airborne Manston 0848 hours 10th October 1944 together with S/Ldr. McCall and F/Lt. Pengelly - landed at STTES Groups 3 East Marseilles for re-fuelling and weather report. Airborne STTES Groups 3East 1340 and landed at IESI, Italy 1630 hours.

Airborne IESI 0920 hours 11th October 1944 and set course over ANCONA for Dalmatian Coast south of SENJ intending to cross the mountains if possible below cloud. We flew north as far as SENJ inside the islands and sought a cloud gap through which to penetrate the mountain barrier. There was no break in the clouds and so we turned out to sea again on a course of 225 degrees M. from SENJ, climbing on the way out and then turning to the reciprocal, still climbing to get over the top of the clouds. A fairly heavy box barrage of flak was put up from an island 10 miles S.W. of SENJ but fortunately it was all below us and no-one was hit.

We continued to climb in an inverted Vic formation, S/Ldr. McCall flying abreast at S/400 yds. to starboard and F/Lt. Pengelly flying astern. We crossed over the mountains and I gave it another very short burst of light, peggily found myself badly positioned and attacking upwards a hangar and so broke off his attack. As I pulled away I saw flames coming from the range of the aerodrome (1030 hours) and dived to commence the attack, calling on the others to follow me. I fired 1½ sec. burst at Me 110 parked on the south side of the aerodrome from the range of the engines. Smoke started to rise from the port mainplane and I gave it another very short burst of cannon and machine gun fire to break off and so broke off before firing. S/Ldr McCall came in to attack it as I broke away and the aircraft was lost sight of the cockpit. This they did after attacking the Me/E/A and, as they left the aerodrome and before they reached the sea several hundred feet high.

We were being engaged by light flak as we broke away from the first attack and I turned steeply to make an attack on the second aircraft. I turned too tightly, found myself below and astern of a hangar and so broke off before firing. S/Ldr McCall came in to attack it as I broke away and the aircraft blew up underneath him sending up a column of smoke several hundred feet high.

As I pulled away I turned to port to see if there was any activity there. There was no flying going on in the area, and as we did not immediately locate the aerodrome so after a brief search we set course for ZAGREB. We approached ZAGREB a/d from due south and I pulled up as we were south of the field to see what targets were available. I saw a Ju 87 and another S/E A/C parked on the south-east corner of the airfield and I commenced an average strike all over the aerodrome. S/Ldr McCall came in to attack it as I broke away and the aircraft put a silk of the cockpit. S/Ldr McCall came in to attack it as I broke away and the aircraft blew up underneath him sending up a column of smoke several hundred feet high.

straight run from 800 feet flying from East to West to get a/c in line. I gave the first a/c a fairly long burst and then moved the sight up to the second one, parked close by. As we passed over them, both were starting to smoke and burn. I broke away sharply to port and as we did so there was a crash in the 'office' and F/Lt. Hatseill said that he had been hit. The flak was getting pretty active and almost at the same moment my port engine appeared to be emitting a long broad stream of white vapour.

Thinking I looked back I could see the smaller fires of the Ju 87's. I an aircraft which S/Ldr. McCall had attacked and the smaller fires of the Ju 87's. I called up the others and told them that we had been hit and should form up and return. We started out to southland to tossed the mountain before our port engine packed up when S/Ldr. McCall reported fighters above and behind us, we therefore dived for earth again, but found them not to be fighters and therefore dived for straight and set a/c fairly low. A few minutes later I found that the white trail from my port engine had stopped, from the port other tank, which had been holed by a cannon shell and that the engine was O.K.

We returned to IESI, where I found that my port tyre had been holed also but as we had anticipated this possibility we were able to carry out a successful landing 1140 hours without any further damage to the aircraft. After landing, it was found that S/Ldr. McCall's engine (star board) had been hit in the sump.

S/Ldr McCall, F/Lt. Hatseil and I returned direct to Manston the next day 0920 hours 12th. October from IESI in the remaining serviceable aircraft. F/Lt. Pengelly is returning with a second aircraft within 24 hours.

CLAIM 1 Me 110 Destroyed. 2 Ju 87's Destroyed.

ARMAMENT REPORT.

	S.A.P.I.	H.E.I.	Brownings.
P.O.	83	83	Nil.
P.I.	83	83	Nil.
S.I.	83	83	Nil.
S.O.	83	83	Nil.

Sgd., R.A. Mitchell, D.F.C., had a .303 type bullet rip open his right flying boot and eventually lodge in the heel of his left boot.

Sgd., L.J.Gibson, F/O,
Intelligence Officer, No. 605 Sqdn.
R.A.F. Station, Manston, KENT.

Sgd., R.A. Mitchell, D.F.C.,
Pilot, No. 605 Squadron,
R.A.F. Station, Manston.

Note:- F/Lt. Mitcell, D.F.C., had a .303 type bullet rip open his right flying boot and eventually lodge in the heel of his left boot.

SECRET.

From: No. 605 (County of Warwick) Squadron, R.A.F., Station, Manston.

To: Headquarters A.D.G.B. (2)., Headquarters No.11 Group (2)., S.I.O. R.A.F. Biggin Hill., Nos. 418 and 29 Squadrons, R.A.F. Hunsdon., No. 60 O.T.U. High Ercall., Intelligence, Manston, I.O. 605 Squadron (8).

Serial No. May/60/39.

PERSONAL COMBAT REPORT.

STATISTICAL.

Date;   (A) 11th. October, 1944.
Unit;   (B) 605 (County of Warwick) Squadron.
Type and mark of aircraft; (C) Mosquito VI.
Time attack was delivered; (D) 1030 - 1035 hours.
Place of attack;   (E) PLESO A/F. (ii) ZAGREB A/F.
Weather;   (F) Excellent visibility. High scattered cloud.
Our casualties - aircraft; (G) Mosquito VI Cat. AC.
               - personnel;   (H) Nil.
Enemy casualties - in air combat; (J) Nil.
               - ground or sea targets; (K) (ii) 1 Destroyed (shared with S/Ldr. McCall.

Pilot. F/Lt. J.I.Pengelly.   Navigator. F/Sgt. G.H.Couchman.

DAY RANGER - BUDAPEST AREA.

Airborne Manston 0848 hours 10th October 1944, together with W/Cdr. Mitchell, D.F.C., and Bar and S/Ldr. McCall. Landed at STTES Groups 3 East for re-fuelling and weather report. Airborne Groups 3 East 1340 and landed IESI Italy 1630 hours.

Airborne IESI 0920 hours 11th October 1944 and set course over ANCONA for Dalmatian coast south of SENJ intending to cross the mountains if possible below cloud. We flew north as far as SENJ inside the islands and sought a cloud gap through which to penetrate the mountain barrier. There was no break in the clouds and so we turned out to sea again on a course of 220 degs. M. from SENJ, climbing on the way out and then turning to the reciprocal, still climbing to get over the top of the clouds. A fairly heavy box barrage of flak was put up from an island 10 miles S.W. of SENJ but fortunately it was all below us and no-one was hit.

We then re-formed to continue our sortie and in doing so looted PLESO airfield where there were aircraft widely dispersed. We followed W/Cdr. Mitchell in and we attacked an Me 109 with a 4 - 5 second burst and found that the plane on the east of the range of buildings set itself. I saw many strikes on the E 7J(believed) I was too late to say my attack had already formed itself. I saw many strikes on the E.711.(believed). W/Cdr. Mitchell also attached this aircraft. It was seen to be burning according S/Ldr McCall and myself each claim ½ E.711 (believed) destroyed.

We continued climbing and flew round to plan formation, many strikes were seen along the wings and across the fuselage and as we passed over the aircraft bits were seen flying off and smoke was seen to be coming from five somewhere in what remained of the mobiles. As we broke away from the airfield W/Cdr. Mitchell called up and said that he had been hit, therefore S/Ldr. McCall (my leader) formed up on him and started his way back to our advance base at IESI, landing at 1140 hours. It was later found that all three Mosquitos had been damaged by light flak.

CLAIM ½ E.711 (believed) destroyed.
1 Me 109 destroyed.

ARMAMENT REPORT.

	S.A.P.I.	H.E.I.	Brownings.
P.O.	84	83	Nil.
P.I.	84	83	Nil.
S.I.	84	85	Nil.
S.O.	84	85	Nil.

Sgd., John I. Pengelly, F/Lt.
Pilot, No. 605 Squadron,
R.A.F. Station, Manston, KENT.

Sgd., L.J.Gibson, F/O,
Intelligence Officer, No. 605 Sqdn.
R.A.F. Station, Manston, KENT.

22 Feb 1945: Operation Clarion

OPERATION "CLARION"
FEB. 1945

On the 22nd. February 1945, the R.A.F. struck a tremendous blow in daylight against Hitler's rapidly dwindling lines of communication in Germany. A maximum effort was called for and 605 put all its available crews and aircraft into the air in 10 minutes.

19 aircraft of the Squadron did their stuff; but only 15 returned. Of these 15, UP/E and UP/V came back on one engine pilotted by F/O Archer and W/O Osborne with Sgt Riley and W/O Read navigating, respectively. Another of the 15, UP/J, pilotted by F/Lt. Rix, D.F.M., returned to belly land as the hydraulics were U/S.

The experiences of S/Ldr I.P.McCall (later D.F.C.) and his navigator, P/O T.Caulfield who were shot down in UP/K, are given in a report below. This crew were repatriated and so was F/Sgt. Hinton, navigator to F/Lt. Enticott who lost his life. Other personnel missing were F/O Owen, P/O Thirlwell, F/Lt. Jones and F/O Phillips and no news of these has come through.

"C" for Charlie after returning from Operation "Clarion" on 22nd. Feb. 1945.

W/O Donaldson pilotted this aircraft safely back to base from Germany in daylight with F/O 'Junior' Allen navigating.
After bombing a town, they straffed a signal box and then turned their attention to a building which they proceeded to well and truly shoot up. In one attack they really pressed home to a close range and in pulling out the starboard wing hit the building with results which can be seen in the photograph. A safe landing was made at base despite the dangling aileron and the useless flap.

"V" for Victory returns from Operation "Clarion" on 22nd. February 1945.

F/O H.B. Archer and his navigator, Sgt. Riley, flew this aircraft back from Germany in daylight on one engine after it had been badly shot up with flak. Previously on this trip they had successfully bombed roads and straffed sheds

W/O G.B.Riley and F/Lt. H.B.Archer.

This crew joined 605 on 20th. Nov. 1944 during the non-operational period that followed the transfer to 2 Group. They took part in the Squadron's first operations with 2 Group and by "VE Day" had successfully completed over 30 sorties. Both saw the end of 605 in Aug. '45.

Their aircraft is shown at the centre on left, after returning on one engine from Germany on 22nd. Feb. '45.

22 Feb 1945: Operation Clarion: S/Ldr Ian McCall D.F.C. : extracts from his story.

SECRET.

Squadron Leader I.F. McCall -
605 Sqdn. P/W -22nd February - 30th March 1945.
Released by Americans 30th March 1945.

S/Ldr. McCall, pilot of an aircraft of 605 Squadron, engaged on operation "Clarion", February 22nd, 1945, was shot down by Flak near to ESTERWEGEN off the KUSTEN CANAL. The following is his story :-

FEBRUARY 22th. Having attacked his target he flew down the KUSTEN CANAL setting a barge on fire and as he pulled up to pass over a bridge and attack another barge the other side, he was hit by 20 m.m. flak in the nose of the aircraft, shattering the Instrument Panel. In swinging round the Mosquito collided with some telegraph wires and a pole which so damaged the port mainplane that S/L. McCall was forced to make a crashlanding at once - in a field nearby. At 13.12 hours, both he and his navigator extricated themselves from the aircraft. S/Ldr. McCall had seven wounds, 4 in the leg, 2 in the arm and one in the back - including a bren arm. The aircraft immediately afterwards caught fire and it is understood from the Huns that nothing was left of it. McCall was picked up by Hitler Youth and a Farm Labourer and taken to the nearest village - about the name of which he is uncertain, and locked up in the local pub. He received no medical attention and was told that there was no Doctor in the vicinity. At 18.30 hours a Flak Officer interviewed him and asked hardly any questions and merely took away a certain amount of his equipment, e.g., escape kits, etc. By midnight a small waggon appeared and took the Pilot and his Navigator to the detention barracks near. Here an Austrian prisoner - medical studen gave McCall a shot of morphia, bandaged the arm, and put him in a dental chair where the Hun guards left the lights on all night shining into his face and refused to let them out. At first the guard would not get any water or give attention. A later guard did produce some water.

FEBRUARY 23rd. On the 23rd, with a temperature, and still no further medical attention they were told to get up and although it was raining were sent out of the Detention Barracks down to a French "lager", which was a private house some 15 kilometres away. This distance they were made to walk. (It is believed that the reason for seeing them out of the village was the fact that a Mosquito had sometime previously killed 15 people when it had attacked the barracks.) On arrival at this house, about mid-day the 23rd, they received their first meal which consisted of some brown bread and later some soup from French prisoners who were billeted there.

FEBRUARY 24th On the 24th a number of villagers came in and from their attitude at first it seemed as if the airmen might be subjected to some violence, but later some older village women arrived bringing them some soup.

FEBRUARY 25th On the 25th, still with a temperature, no sleep and loss of blood and though the arm was swelling up considerably, they were told to go to the nearest railhead. Communications were in a chaotic state - no telephone and trains running anyhow. 3 guards procured a horse and cart and drove them in this for about 50 kilos. As they passed through the village there was a considerable amount of shouting and anger by the children but the older women did not behave in this way. At dark a stretcher was obtained and they were taken from MEPPEN to LINGEN, where, on visiting the control point they were referred to by the Huns as "English swine", and taken to the nearby hospital. Here a Captain Madoux, a French prisoner of war, who had been there for 3 years did everything he could for them. There was no staff, no medical equipment and very little attention. Food consisted of 3 slices of black bread per day with two tins of acorn coffee, one at night, one in the morning, and occasionally soup which was so revolting that the majority of people could hardly stomach it. For three weeks McCall remained here. The hospital gradually filled with German casualties coming from the Russian front and approximately March 15th, the guards were told to take McCall to Frankfurt. (F/O Caulfield(McCall's navigator) had been sent on to Frankfurt after the second night at LINGEN.

Continued 2

- 2 -

MARCH 15th - 21st. He was given a loaf of black bread and half a German Sausage which was to last the whole journey. The Senior Guard said that had he seen McCall when he came out of the aircraft he would certainly have shot him ("A murderer who beat up and killed women and children") and in any case the guard did not expect him (McCall) to get into FRANKFURT alive owing to the attitude of the civilians. The following is the route to FRANKFURT which took six days and five nights :

LINGEN - RHEINE - MUNSTER - OSNABRUCK - BRACKERDE -
HAMM - PADERBORN - KASSEL - MARBURG - GIESSEN -
FRANKFURT - OBERURSEL.

There was a complete lack of any organisation, no attempt to get them to a P.O.W. Camp quickly: the guards instructions were - "Frankfurt is their destination, get them there the best way you can" - and it did not appear to matter whether it took them two days or two weeks. Throughout, no consideration was given to the fact that they were prisoners of war or that McCall was in a very serious state. This in spite of repeated protests. On the day they set out they had missed the train and had to wait until 4 o'clock in the morning in the open for the next train. One of the guards attempted to give them a bowl of soup from the Red Cross Station but was told by a soldier that if he tried any of that foolishness, he'd see he had six months in jail. On arrival at MUNSTER the line and conditions were so bad they had to return to OSNABRUCK where, with the frost on the ground they spent the night. McCall only had a vest, shirt and thin waistcoat and his battle dress thrown over his arm. The whole journey was made partially by train, partially by walking and occasionally by road transport.

In the OSNABRUCK area they were put in a box car behind the engine and when the train stopped for air raid warnings and the rest of the people jumped into the banks they were locked in so that they couldn't escape. (Another trick of the Huns was to place people in a Red Cross car with a small red cross on the side and put this between a flak waggon and an ammo. truck and then when strafed by our own people to say that we took no notice of the Red Cross Rules). No distance in the train lasted more than 30 - 40 kilos. before a stop where changes had to be made because the line was up. At KASSEL they walked from one side of the town for seven miles through the town in order to get a connection. At MARLBURG in their walk through the town, civilians threw bricks and wanted to lynch them. Although incidents of this kind happened at other places, this was the worst. One night was spent in a forest - another under a railway engine in KASSEL - others on platforms and only very occasionally was any shelter provided.

'J' for Johnnie, safely home after Operation 'Clarion' on 22nd February 1945. F/Lt Rix, D.F.M., with F/O Burrows navigating bombed a railway junction and destroyed a railway engine with cannon fire before they were badly hit by flak and the hydraulic system put out of action. They returned to base where F/Lt Rix executed a masterly belly landing which was described as a 'treat to watch'. The aircraft being fitted with paddle-blade propellers, he correctly came in and neatly feathered the port engine just before settling down. As can be seen this did not prevent the prop coming off but it did not hit the fuselage and neither of the crew were injured.

'A' Flight at Coxyde, Belgium in March 1945.

Front row, left to right;- F/O W.J.Beney, Sgt. A.W.Davies, F/O D.E.Hutchinson, F/Lt. F.E.A. Quinn. M.B.E., F/O E.G.Lendon, Sgt. H.I.Parsons, F/O Mann (Intell. Off.).
Second row, left to right;- F/Lt. J.G.Harrison, F/Lt. R.Moon, F/O M.B.Hickling, F/Lt. P.P. Middleton (Deputy Flight Commander), S/Ldr. C.F.Ponsford (later D.F.C.,), F/Lt. A.V.Rix. D.F.M., F/Lt. A.N.Biscoe, F/Lt. E.K.Pallis (R.C.A.F.,), F/Sgt. P.B.Thompson.
Third row, left to right;- L/A/C's Smerdon, Harris, Warner, Smith. Cpl. Staniland, Sgt. 'Slash' Phillips, F/Sgt. Ritchie (later 'mentioned'-), Cpl. Gibbons, Sgt. Fairman, L/A/C's Dinnecombe, Pyfield.
Fourth row, left to right;- L/A/C's Marshall, Foster, Mills, Wem, Davies, Sparks, Hayward, Smith, Day, McGowan, Jones, Duncan, Norton, Eldidge, ? (M.T.), Bullman and Chamberlain.
On Mossie, F/O G.H.Allen, F/O R.Burrows, F/O A.H.Jackson (R.C.A.F.,).

April 1944: 605's "official" crest is approved.

At the celebration dinner many old members were interested to see for the first time the squadron badge, which was registered in 1942 shortly before the present squadron was reformed after taking part in operations in Java. The badge consists of the Warwickshire "Bear and Ragged Staff" in the standard R.A.F. surround.

The motto is "Nunquam Dormio" - "I Never Sleep". Its adoption has an interesting origin. During the first nine years of its existence, the squadron went to Manston, Kent, for its annual camp. Pleasure was combined with business; for many members of that squadron it was their only yearly holiday. Returning in the small hours to camp one morning some convivial spirits found an evening newspaper poster which read "Sleep is just a waste of time". The poster was duly framed and hung for many years in the mess at Castle Bromwich. The motto originated from these words and was, in fact, singularly apt, for the squadron has turned during the war from the role of day fighters to night intruders.

26/8/45: F/O Arturo Linn DFC & S/Ldr Arthur Woods DFC by cannon on UP-Y

1945: 605 Mosquito RS529 at Coxyde

Sept 1945: 605 Adjutant F/O Charlie Beech undergoing a medical inspection from the Squadron Doc

1945: 605 aircrew at Volkel, Holland. Extreme right is Sid Hudson, behind Bill Jones (in wellies). S/Ldr Arthur Woods with cigarette in middle.

1945: F/Lt John Worthington D.F.C.(in truck) & F/O Alan Friar D.F.C.

June 1945: 605 Mosquito UP-U SZ967 at Volkel

Clay pigeon shooting from an old bomb crater on the drome at Volkel, Holland. This was a popular pastime during the summer of 1945. From left to right:- F/Lt. H.H.Proud, F/Lt. A.E.Biscoe, F/O A.Lendon.

F/O D.E.Hutchinson and F/Lt.J.G.Harrison.
"Hutch" arrived with 605 on the 3rd. of December '44 as navigator to F/O M.B.Hickling and together they saw VE day, with 605, after which Mike Hickling was posted and "Hutch" crewed up with various pilots.
Jim Harrison was posted in on the 4th. April '45 with P/O W.J.Beney as navigator. In a week they were operating and by VE Day they had completed 9 Ops. Jim (seated in the 'snap') later became Deputy Flight Commander 'A' Ft. and he, Bill Beney and 'Hutch' all saw the end of 605 with the Squadron.

Sept 1945: 605, Pheasant Plucking

1 Sept 1945: S/Ldr Colin Ponsford D.F.C. & S/Ldr Arthur Woods D.F.C. & Bar with their bag for the day, in front of their 5-star accommodation at Volkel.

Sept 1945: S/Ldr Colin Ponsford D.F.C. & F/Lt Frank Quinn with their ground-crew

1945: A 605 airman and a German captured French tank!

26/8/45: S/Ldr Arthur Woods D.F.C. & Bar with his Mosquito UP-Y "Get Up Them Stairs. Note the Flight Commander's flash under the German Swastikas.

VE Day 1945: 605 ground-crew posing for a photograph in front of one of the Squadron's Mosquitos

May 45: S/Ldr Arthur Woods D.F.C. & Bar outside 605's Hut at Volkel. The name "Arthur's Joint" can be seen written on the prop blade above the door.

8 May 45 'VE Day': 605 celebrating Victory in Europe Day with a beer.

Lest We Forget

Oldenburg New Cemetery;- a crew side by side in their last resting place.

F/Lt. Andrews (Pilot) and Sgt. Freeman (Navigator) failed to return from an intruder sortie on the night of the 26th. Sept. 1944. They set out to patrol Varrelbusch and Ahlhorn airfields where the Hun based his He 111's which at this time were carrying pilotless aircraft ('divers' or 'buzz-bombs') to the North Sea where they would release them at low level directed over East Anglia.

F/Lt. Andrews joined the R.A.F. in April 1940 and instructed in England and Canada before joining the Squadron on the 15th. August 1944.

Sgt. Freeman joined the R.A.F. in March 1941 and remustered from a ground trade in Oct.'41. He was trained in England and Canada and joined 605 on 15th. Aug.'44.

Together they completed six operations - and failed to return from their seventh, just six weeks after joining the Squadron.

Nine crews of 605 intruded on the night of 26th/27th Sept.'44 - of these nine, three went to Varrelbusch and Ahlhorn and one came back. The crew was S/Ldr. L.W.Welch. D.F.C., and Bar and F/O L.R.Page. D.F.M., and Bar - they reported much Searchlight activity and very accurate flak - visibility poor - Ahlhorn airfield lit.

The other missing crew was F/Lt. Storer and F/Sgt. Lees and they were on their fifteenth operation.

In a wood near Arnhem, Holland, a crew of 605 lie buried with the wreckage of their Mosquito a few feet away. For a wreath one grave bears the remains of the safety straps and parachute harness; the other mound is covered with a map and a flying helmet crowns the cross.

On the 9th. November 1944, F/Lt. R.M.Singer (Pilot) and his navigator, F/O I.C.Redgersen took off from Manston aerodrome at 2030 hours to intrude and patrol Arderf and Marx aerodromes in N.W.Germany. They were New Zealanders and had joined the Squadron on the 27th. June 1944. They did not return from this sortie.

Months later when the advancing Allied armies had liberated Holland their graves were located and photographed.

May 1946: 605 is re-formed.

BIRMINGHAM SQUADRON REVIVED
No. 605 will be night fighters

RECRUITING begins to-day for the Auxiliary Air Force, fighting air arm whose week-end fliers six years ago laid down tools in their civilian jobs and in a few short months were helping to smash the weight of the Luftwaffe over London.

It is a rare tribute to the value of the A.A.F. that the Air Ministry should be reviving it again so soon after the end of the war.

Altogether, 20 squadrons are planned for the new A.A.F. They will consist of four squadrons of light bombers, 13 of day fighters and three of night fighters.

All the units will be equipped with operational aircraft, fighters for the present having Spitfires and the light bombers and night fighters Mosquitos.

The No. 605 (County of Warwick) squadron — so often regarded as Birmingham's own because of the number of Birmingham men who served in it—figures in the plans as a night-fighter

"WEEK-END AIR FORCE" TRAIN AT HONILEY
County of Warwick Squadron Plans

COUNTY of Warwick Squadron of the Auxiliary Air Force— the "Week-end Air Force"—has been allocated R.A.F. Station, Honiley, near Kenilworth, for training purposes with night-fighter Mosquito aircraft.

Although recruiting of Auxiliaries only began this week, already more than 60 Warwickshire men have expressed a wish to join. At the moment recruiting of men is confined to former R.A.F. personnel now demobilised. It is intended to make the Squadron a front line home defence unit.

Castle Bromwich Aerodrome —original "home" of the Squadron—will be used only for ground instructional purposes on week-day evenings, but flying will be carried out on Saturdays and Sundays at Honiley, which is now fully equipped with permanent staff to cater for a large intake of men who want to join, either as flyers or ground crews.

"EVERY COMFORT"

Young, bemedalled "Permanent Adjutant" of the Squadron, Flight Lieutenant D. Giles, told a "Coventry Standard" reporter that men who had served in all trades of the R.A.F. would be welcomed to the Squadron.

"Transport will be provided from all centres of the county, and we are going to see that Auxiliaries get every comfort," he said.

"They will sleep in former W.A.A.F. billets on Saturday nights and sheets will be provided. None of the old '40 to a hut' system about this station for Auxiliaries. We want to provide a good fellowship club, as well as do a job of work."

Group Captain J. A. Cecil Wright, A.F.C., T.D., D.L., who formed the original Squadron (known officially as No. 605 Squadron), visited Honiley on Wednesday and met Major A. J. Masterson (Warwickshire Territorial Army and Air Force Association), who is managing the recruiting.

The Commanding Officer of the Squadron will be an Auxiliary Officer. It is understood that an appointment has not yet been made.

WAR-TIME RECORD

The Auxiliary Air Force—a special Reserve of Home Defence Squadrons—was brought into being in 1924, and the County of Warwick Squadron was formed in 1926 at Castle Bromwich. During the war the Squadron lost some of its local "colour" owing to the inevitable posting of personnel to other R.A.F. duties, but the Air Ministry now wishes to renew local links.

The Squadron consisted of 29 pilots when mobilised in September, 1939. Of these 11 were killed in action or on active service. Two became prisoners of war, and one became a bomber pilot and reached Squadron Leader rank.

The Squadron destroyed 167 enemy aircraft in the war (97 since reforming), probably destroyed 26, and damaged more than 130 others. Crews of the Squadron also destroyed 75 "Flying Bombs." In addition, hundreds of trains, locomotives, barges and motor vehicles have been accounted for by the Squadron.

1947: CO S/Ldr Walker DSO (centre, hand in pocket) with members of 605's aircrew and groundcrews

1947: The First Crews: Pilots and Navigators in front of one of the Squadron's Mosquito NF.36 aircraft.

Winter 1947: Main Gate at RAF Honiley after a large snowfall that was common during a particularly harsh Winter.

1947: A ground crew member covers up a Mosquito engine as a formation flies overhead.

1947: Refuelling a Mosquito on the line opposite the control tower at Honiley.

1948: A group of 605 airmen, the backbone of any Squadron, and 605 were blessed with an exceptional bunch.

1948: Line-up of Mosquitos at RAF Honiley

July 1948: Summer Camp at Tangmere: Mosquito NF.36 NT325

July 1948: Some of the lads enjoying a well-deserved pint on an outing from Summer Camp at Tangmere

1947: Some of the first aircrew and ground crew members of the newly formed 605 Squadron at Honiley. CO S/Ldr Walker D.S.O. (9th from the left).

1947: One of 605's two Harvards, KF160

1947: Spitfire Mk TE3? taxiing at Honiley in front of one of 605's Harvards and a line-up of Mosquitos.

1948: Sgts Mess at Honiley

1948: Cpl R. Gardner with 605 Mascot "Prince"

1948: Commanding Officer S/Ldr Ron Goodwin and F/Lt John Timmis (on wing) returning from a flight in one of the Squadron's two Harvards. John took over command of 605 from Ron in July 49.

1948: Group of "regular" airmen with 605 Mascot "Prince" at Honiley.

Old and new at Honiley. 605 (County of Warwick) Auxiliary Squadron's first Vampire jet fighter planes which replace the older Mosquitos seen in the background.

Honiley Receives First Jet Fighters

605 SQUADRON EQUIPPED FOR NEW ROLE

Four Vampire jet fighters, the first of 10 to be supplied to 605 (County of Warwick) Auxiliary Squadron, have arrived at Honiley, the squadron's base, and training on them begins officially this week-end.

The unit, previously equipped with Mosquitoes, thus become the first auxiliary squadron to be fitted with these Goblin-powered aircraft, and a factor which has weighed heavily in the Air Ministry's considerations in making the allotment has been the 2,000-yard runway at Honiley, which is 400 yards longer than the specified safety distance for jet aircraft.

The arrival of the Vampires coincides with the appointment of Squadron Leader R. C. T. Goodwin, formerly a Flight Commander at commanding officer of 605. The filling of this position has been the squadron's biggest problem since it was re-formed after the war, and has been a handicap which has kept it behind other auxiliary squadrons in progress.

Honily is also to be one of the first stations to be granted auxiliary air controllers when recruiting is opened for this branch in the near future.

Change-Over

The squadron is now passing officially from night interception, for which it earned a distinguished reputation during the war, back to day fighting. The pilots are undergoing conversion courses on Harvards and Spitfires, and then will "go off" on the single-seater Vampires.

The navigators in the crews of the discarded Mosquitos are to be partly absorbed in administrative duties and partly disbanded. The main problem is still one of ground crews in all trades—the present strength is 65, and there is urgent need for twice that number. Flying hours are being restricted by lack of men to service the aircraft.

From now on, villagers in this area of Warwickshire will be familiar with the vibrant whine of the jets. Flight-Lieutenant J. C. Button, D.S.O. D.F.C., the squadron adjutant made low level flights over the airfield to-day, and the turf around the dispersal points is already scorched yellow and brown.

Conversion Not Difficult

The conversion from piston engines to jet handling is not difficult (writes "The Birmingham Mail" air correspondent).

In the air the aircraft responds smoothly to the controls and only the landing approach requires extra caution — the power is slower in response to throttle movement in cases of overshooting, while, when the throttle is closed completely, there is still thrust from the unit which prolongs the landing run and which can only be safeguarded by careful breaking. The Vampires are armed with four cannon.

Summer 1948: 605 gained the distinction of being the first Auxiliary Squadron to receive jet aircraft. The Mossies made way for the de Havilland Vampire F.1.

Summer 1948: F/Lt Johnny Button D.S.O. D.F.C arrives over Tangmere in 605's first Vampire

28 July 1948: 605 are honoured with the Granting of the Freedom of Entry into the Borough of Stratford-upon-Avon

VITAL NEED FOR T.A. INSTRUCTORS

FAR TOO FEW COMING FORWARD —FIELD MARSHAL MONTGOMERY

STRATFORD HONOURS THREE COUNTY UNITS

Field Marshal Viscount Montgomery, chairman of the Permanent Military Defence Committee, for the West, called for more volunteer instructors for the Territorial Army when he spoke at Stratford-on-Avon to-day. Far too few were coming forward, he said.

Lord Montgomery was addressing troops and Midland dignitaries in the crowded Bridge Street after the borough had conferred freedom of entry to Stratford upon the Royal Warwickshire Regiment, the Warwickshire Yeomanry and the County of Warwick Fighter Squadron of the Royal Auxiliary Air Force.

Lord Montgomery, who is Colonel-in-Chief of the Royal Warwickshire Regiment, was acknowledging the honour done the Regiment. Lord Willoughby de Broke represented the Warwickshire Yeomanry and Air Commodore Cecil Wright the 605 Fighter Squadron.

Lord Montgomery said: "The Territorial Army is the framework upon which the National Army depends, and it is vital that it should be able to meet its commitments. At the present time it is busy building up its cadres of volunteer instructors, who must be ready to receive the first intake of National Service men. These National Service men having completed their 12 months with the colours will start to flow into the T.A. in January, 1950, and volunteer instructors are badly needed."

Thanking the borough for "the great honour you have done my regiment," Lord Montgomery said, "I regarded the Second Battalion as one of the best in my group of armies."

The regiment had maintained a close association with Stratford for a great many years and had not forgotten that Charles Dibden's song, "Ye Warwickshire Lads and Ye Lasses" was first sung in Stratford's streets.

"That occurred in 1769 at the first large-scale celebrations held there in honour of Shakespeare. Then, years later, the Regiment adopted the song as its regimental march and keeps it to this day."

605 Squadron "Flies past"

Lord Montgomery took the salute at a march past which followed the ceremony, with the band of the Royal Warwickshire Regiment playing. Aircraft of the 605 Squadron "flew past" and tanks of the Yeomanry rumbled through Bridge Street, Wood Street, Greenhill Street to the sale ground. Other troops marched through the town along the longer route.

In presenting illuminated copies of the Town Council's resolutions conferring the freedom on the three units, the Mayor of Stratford (Lt.-Col. Fordham Flower) said it was a measure of the Borough's gratitude for the distinguished and heroic part they have played in the defence of their families and their homes, of their land and of their liberty; not only during the most recent world struggle, but ever since they were raised and founded.

"Meanwhile, none of us mus—

"Have then the sagas and the sacrifices that we honour to-day been all in vain?" continued the Mayor. "If we affirm that the day of voluntary service and individual sacrifice is over, then the answer, alas—and to our eternal shame—is yes, and our ceremony this afternoon is nothing more than lip service to these three units and an empty tribute to the sons of Stratford who for many generations past have fought and died in their ranks."

"Let us rather match these Deeds of Privilege with other deeds—deeds of service. Let us go forth again to help fill gaps in the ranks of the Warwickshire land and air forces. The gratitude and pride and the admiration we express to-day are hollow sentiments unless we are prepared to shoulder our share of our country's defence by helping to restore the county regiments and the county squadron to their full state of strength and effectiveness."

"Physical forces of an immensity before undreamed are at man's beck and call, for better or maybe for worse. We face to-day a prospect more sinister, more dangerous, more terrifying than that which confronted us 10 years ago.

"Hollow sentiments, unless—"

CONFERMENT OF THE FREEDOM OF ENTRY INTO THE BOROUGH.

28 July 1948 — The Royal Warwickshire Regiment.
28 July 1948 — The Warwickshire Yeomanry.
28 July 1948 — Number 605 (County of Warwick) Fighter Squadron Royal Auxiliary Air Force.
25 April 1959 — The Corps of Royal Engineers.

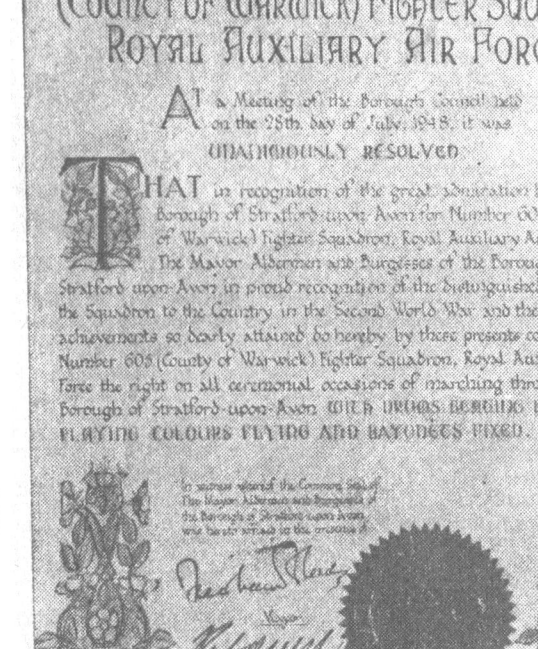

This illuminated deed of privilege was handed to Air-Commodore J. A. Cecil Wright for No. 605 (County of Warwick) fighter squadron, R.A.A.F. at the Stratford cerem to-day.

One of No. 605 Squadron's two Meteor Mark VII jet aircraft, with F/Lt. P. J. Anson, chief flying instructor, getting in the cockpit. Behind him is F/Lt. H. A. Asker, squadron adjutant.

Meteors At Honiley

"605's" ACQUISITION

No. 605 (County of Warwick) Squadron, which was the first Auxiliary unit to be equipped with Vampires, the de Havilland jet-powered aircraft, has now received important additions to its flying strength with the arrival of two Meteor Mark VII jets.

The two-seater Meteors are at Honiley to give squadron pilots instrument flying practice, which presents special problems in aircraft with a top speed of more than 600 m.p.h. and a climbing rate of 8,000 feet a minute.

They are used also for converting experienced pilots of piston-engined aircraft to jet flying.

An increase in numbers, both of pilots and ground crew, has followed recruiting efforts, which have been stimulated by the introduction of measures to make training at Honiley easier. Special buses are now run from Birmingham for week-end training, and a squadron rest room has been added to the social facilities.

1949: Ray Raby (standing), ? and Norman Devonport

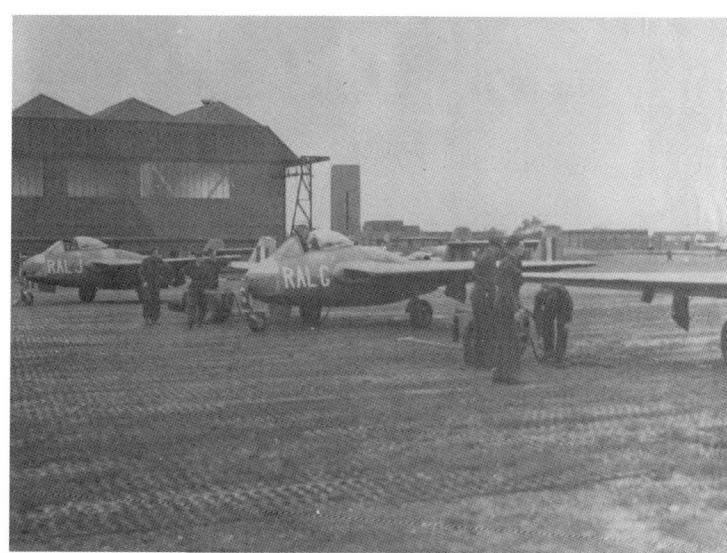

400 m.p.h. IN JET WAS A PLEASURE

"We are now over Birmingham ... and ... this ... is .. Wolverhampton ... coming up to starboard."

THAT sentence, read reasonably slowly, will tell you almost exactly the time taken by a jet fighter to travel from the Midland metropolis across the murk of the Black Country to Wolverhampton at a very moderate cruising speed.

That, too, was my experience yesterday, writes an *Express and Star* reporter, when I was flown from Honily aerodrome, near Birmingham, in a new Meteor VII twin-seat jet trainer recently delivered to 605 (County of Warwick) Squadron, Royal Auxiliary Air Force.

LATEST TRAINER

The Meteor VII is the R.A.F.'s latest training aircraft, an aircraft to cut down the laborious stages from primary training to jet-fighter flight as part of a new system of training.

Before the Gloster Aircraft Co. developed the Meteor VII, no pilot had any chance of dual control training on a jet fighter. His stages were primary training on the venerable Tiger Moth, faster piston engine flying on dual control Harvards, even faster flying on Spitfires and then the lone adventure in a Meteor.

Now the course is considerably shortened and from the Harvard auxiliary pilots go straight to jet flight in the Meteor VII.

ADVENTUROUS STEP

Although they are more used to flying than I was the change from Harvard to Meteor is an adventurous step to them, just as my flight yesterday ranked as an adventure that few people outside the R.A.F. ever have the pleasure of experiencing.

IT WAS A PLEASURE

It was a pleasure, no matter how uncomfortable you on the ground might think it to be to be hurtling through the air at upwards of 400 m.p.h.

Once I was settled in the Meteor comfortably seated on my parachute, carefully keeping my hands and feet away from anything that might upset our progress, and Flight-Lieutenant Asker started his two jet motors, everything was as pleasant as possible.

Taxi-ing, using brakes and a little engine—the jet turbines were turning over at a comfortable 30,000 revolutions—was just like riding in a well-sprung car.

SENSATIONS BEGIN—

Sensations really begin at the take-off. The revolution counters connected to the turbines race round their dials to show some tremendous speed. An unseen force pushes you well into your seat and in no time—literally in seconds—the air speed indicator is showing over 300 miles an hour and you are circling the aerodrome at 3,000 feet.

AND END—

I might have written that sensations also end with the take-off, for in straight and level flight at a cruising speed of some 400 miles an hour there is literally no sensation and the ground crawls past underneath at an incredibly slow speed.

It is only when you realise that you are now travelling at 400 miles an hour 7,000 feet above the ground that you left less than a minute ago that the difference between jet flight and any other form of flying becomes phenomenal.

BUT ONE MORE EXPERIENCE

Out of deference to my inexperience of jet flight my pilot refrained from executing some of those amazing evolutions of which the Meteor is capable. But there was one more experience in the bag, the application of dive brakes to slow down the Meteor when coming in to land.

The dive brakes go down, your stomach performs yet a new motion, the Meteor shudders and is slowed down to between 150 and 200 miles an hour by an invisible but very powerful hand.

AND THE PILOT LOVES IT

And the pilot's version of all this? He just revels in it. The Meteor is an easy aeroplane to fly. Too easy, perhaps, for the safety of new pilots, because in the words of one experienced instructor "You must be 200 per cent. efficient to fly a Meteor. When anything happens it happens quickly."

1949: Vampire F1s RAL-J and RAL-G in front of one of the main hangars at Honiley

25 April 1948: A "full inspection" by AOC No 63 Group A/Cdr "Tiny" Vasse CBE, seen here talking to F/O Hugh Louden at RAF Honiley.

1949: Standing L-R: ?, Hugh Louden, Pete Cope, Arthur Asker, Ray Raby, H. Taylor, Martin Walton, ?, Denis Monk.
Seated L-R: John Timmis, Ron Goodwin (CO) & Johnny Button

1949: 605's first overseas trip, Summer Camp at RAF Sylt, a small island close to the Denmark/Germany border.

4 Jun 1950: F/Lt Martin Walton competes in the Cooper Trophy. Pictured above is his Vampire F1 TG427 NR-H at Honiley.

1950: Squadron Gloster Meteor T7 with airmen

1950: 605 Vampire with a Hastings and 4 Dakotas at Honiley, in readiness to transport the Squadron to Summer Camp at RAF Horsham St Faith in Norfolk.

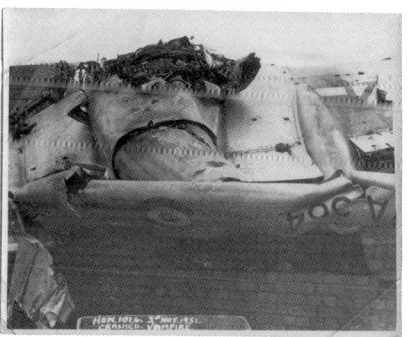

Early 50s: Control Tower at RAF Honiley

1950: CO S/Ldr Johnny Timmis (in cockpit) talking to Honorary Air Commodore, and 605's first CO, A/Cdr Alan Cecil Wright AFC TD, during one of his many visits to the Squadron at Honiley.

3 Nov 1951: The remains of Bill Belcher's Vampire FB5 WA364 at Honiley. Bill's aircraft had suffered an hydraulic failure in flight and he had to force land his Vampire. Amazingly Bill was thrown clear on impact and was uninjured.

A GLIMPSE BEHIND THE SCENES AT HONILEY JET-FIGHTER STATION

Most Pilots Are National Service Men but Wartime Flyers Also Join In

EVERY Sunday thousands of people—and not only the younger generation—lift their heads at the familiar whine of the jet-fighters from Honiley aerodrome and envy the freedom of the pilots, high over the Warwickshire towns and fields. Certainly there can be nothing more exhilarating than flying modern fighters—no better change from the routine of the office than to sally forth into the countryside at Honiley into the R.A.F. atmosphere.

But this week-end flying is, basically, a very serious business. No. 605 Auxiliary Squadron, with its counterparts all over the country provide a considerable portion of the nation's fighter strength, which, hydrogen bombs or not, is of vital importance.

There is a comprehensive training programme to be carried out. Flying "jets" at operational standard is no easy job and the physical strain is such that there is an age limit of 23 on new entrants to the squadron. There are still many

By H. N. Parker

of the "old hands" with hundreds of hours of wartime flying to their credit who have been "converted" from Spitfires or one of the older type and are keeping their hand in.

But more and more of those who have achieved their "wings" during their National Service are coming into the squadron to be carefully trained up to the high standards required. Flight Lieut. P. J. Anson, the flying instructor, has a heavy task on his hands and a rainy week-end is a minor disaster.

Another Side

There is another side to the squadron's life—the unending job of keeping the aircraft in the air. As with the flying personnel of the squadron, there is on the ground staff side a regular nucleus of tradesmen who service the machines in preparation for the week-end's flights.

Here, however, a serious problem arises. There is a shortage of auxiliary ground staff—the men who come out at the week-end—and the squadron has only about half the required number. The cares of home and family keep many ex-R.A.F. men away and, with good wages in civilian life, the full pay is not the inducement it might be. So the R.A.F. is looking to cap the younger generation, and in particular to the young enthusiasts who have already shown their keenness by joining the Air Training Corps. The scheme is to bring these boys out at the week-end to the station to give them experience which will be of great help to them in their period of National Service. After that, they can return as auxiliary ground crews to a station where they are already members of the team.

R.A.F. Regiment

No. 605 Squadron is not, of course, the only feather in Honiley's cap. There is a very keen group of men, many of whom were formerly in the R.A.F. Regiment and these also come out at the week-end to man No. 2605 Light A.A. Squadron, an auxiliary unit equipped with Bofors guns for aerodrome defence. Pilots from all over the country attend a Reserve Command Instrument Training Flight and there is a considerable station staff which keeps the many aspects of the work at Honiley on top line during the week.

All the public sees of Honiley is the jet-fighters overhead at the week-end. But a great deal of work goes into putting them there and into creating a live unit of the Air Force upon the efficiency of which so much depends.

Four Coventry boys at work on one of the latest fighter-aircraft at Honiley. Left to right, Cpl. L. W. Porter, Cpl. C. Radford, L.A.C. S. Hogg and A.C. Bayliss.

June 1950: Summer Camp at Horsham St Faith, Norfolk

June 1950: A/Cdr and 1st CO Alan Cecil Wright (2nd left) with 605 pilots, on one of his many informal visits.

1950: Formation of 605 Vampire F.1s. L-R: RAL-?, VF/279, TG/424 NR-G & TG427 NR-H.

1951: Despite a couple of forced landings, 605 prided itself on an extremely high safety record.

Pilot Crash-lands

Jet Down in Field

A "WEEK-END" R.A.F. flier crash-landed his Vampire jet fighter near the Severn Wild Fowl Trust yesterday and escaped with only a few minor scratches.

He is F/O. Hubert Lowdon, who was on a training flight with two other Vampires from Honiley, Warwickshire, when he developed engine trouble.

F-O. Lowdon managed to bring the plane down in a field at Tanhouse Farm, Frampton-on-Severn, near the parish church. The machine skidded across the field and was severely damaged as it crashed into a ditch.

The pilot went to the farm to telephone and was later flown back to base in another aircraft.

The farmer's wife, Mrs. C. R. Williams, told the "Evening World": "He complained of injuries to his back and I wanted to call a doctor but he said he would wait."

Men and machines await the 'Beware' call

A war-time state of readiness is being kept throughout the first week-end phase of the ten-day exercise "Beware," in which the picture above shows pilots being briefed by the C.O. of No. 605 Squadron, Squadron Leader P. R. M. Walton (right), at Honiley R.A.F. Station.

Round the big camouflaged tents at one end of the runway, the pilots of three squadrons lounge about in their flying kit, dawdling away the sunshine minutes until they are "scrambled." They had been on duty since dawn, and Squadron Leader Walton is re-arranging their battle formation.

Suddenly from the blue sky came the tearing noise of jet engines, and four Vampire fighters wheeled round the aerodrome in a tight circle and peeled off to land rapidly on the runway. It was a flight of 605 Squadron back from a morning interception patrol. Scarcely had they got their Vampires into their parking places in the gleaming line of jet fighters, when there was another alarm.

With two loud explosions and two streaks of flame as the cartridges started their engines into a roar, and two of the fleet, swept-wing Hunters moved out of the line of waiting fighters with a roar and a whistle, they were gone down the runway, and within 30 seconds of the alarm they were airborne.

The Hunter pilots were in a state of immediate readiness with at least two men sitting in the cockpits of the plane ready for instant action.

Meanwhile, 613 Squadron, another volunteer squadron with its headquarters at Manchester, were relaxing around their tent after their efforts earlier in the morning.

Another whistle, and roar, and down came two more of the Hunters rehearsing the destruction of a lone Canberra sneak raider. Within three minutes of their landing they were being refuelled ready for the next emergency.

All over the Midlands, too, other volunteer members of the Royal Observer Corps were taking part in the exercise. A Birmingham furniture manufacturer, Black Country schoolteachers, and Midland farmers had all been up early to man their posts in the system which has its Midland headquarters at Coventry.

One of their biggest tasks is to watch for raiders attempting to slip under the national radar screen in zero-feet hedge-hopping flights.

The Air Ministry reported that the defence in the exercise had been successful against the main threat.

Some of the Hawker Hunters lined up ready for take-off.

Early 1950s: Christmas in the Officers Mess at RAF Honiley.

1951: 605 was adept at all manner of formations.

1952: FREEDOM OF ENTRY INTO THE CITY OF COVENTRY

3 May 1952: 605 were honoured by the City of Coventry, when the Conferment of Freedom of Entry was made by the City Council and the then Lord Mayor Councillor Harry Weston JP. Pictured left is the original citation, with four silver tankards and the Coventry Rose Bowl, which was awarded annually to honour the outstanding Squadron airman.

3 May 1952: S/Ldr Martin Walton leads the Squadron in a march past in front of the Lord Mayor at the Council House in Coventry, and below at the Butts in Coventry.

3 May 1952: A proud moment as a formation of 7 605 Vampires fly over the Council House in Coventry.

1953: Vampire FB5's in formation: WA329 NR-G, VZ336 NR-L, WA358 NR-B, WA360 NR-H and WA458 NR-D

1953: 605 Vampires with visiting aircraft at Honiley.

1954: F/Lt David Waite gets ready for another sortie.

1954: Civilian clerk Joan Peace with F/Lt Mike Scarrott, Regular Adjutant. Joan was affectionately referred to as "Her".

1954: F/O Don Seargent, F/O Ken Cory-Wright, F/O Jerry Edgerton & F/Lt David Waite. Jerry was the last man to fly a 605 sortie in Jan 1957.

1954: PRESENTATION OF THE SQUADRON STANDARD

11 March 1954: HRH Princess Margaret arriving at the main gate at RAF Honiley to present 605 with their Squadron Standard. Regular Adjutant F/Lt Mike Scarrott on left with sword.

605 Standard Bearer P/O Derek John.

HRH Princess Margaret's address: "Squadron Leader Walton, I am very proud to be here today and to have the opportunity of presenting this standard which the Queen has awarded to 605 (County of Warwick) Squadron. During the clouded days of the last war the youngest of our armed forces proved itself to be one of our greatest, and the Squadron which you command won renown remembered far beyond it's native country. In the Battle of Britain, in the Middle East and far across Western Europe it forged a great tradition and we remember with pride and thankful hearts such courage and sacrifice. Now that the war is over, the Squadron does not rest upon it's hard won laurels but still fixes it's gaze upon the years ahead. The pace and scope of invention increases daily, making new demands on your technical ability. But although science has given man mastery of the air, there is one thing that scientific discovery alone can never give. That is the gallantry and spirit of adventure of the men who fly these great machines.

Auxiliary squadrons comprise a new citizen air force on which the Royal Air Force relies for it's support today and on which, should some new emergency arise, may depend the existence of this Realm. For should war come again our country can never hope for a breathing space in which to assemble its reserves and in which to complete their training.

When we listen to the roar of jet engines speeding across the weekend sky we realise the hours of time, and leisure so ungrudgingly given not only by those whom we see for an instant high above us in the skies but also by the ground crews on whose skill and perseverance depends their lives and ours. Your motto is "We never sleep". That is a noble pledge of service, a pledge worthy of Warwick and of England. I present you with this standard, confident that you will guard it with valour in war and with that unswerving devotion in peace which is for ever our best defence."

CO S/Ldr Martin Walton's reply to HRH Princess Margaret's address: "We are very grateful and proud that the occasion has been graced by the presence of your Royal Highness. Your coming here today will make a most memorable occasion in the history of the Squadron. I am sure it is the ambition of all the officers and airmen serving today to deserve the glory and honour obtained for the Squadron by those past comrades in arms, and to match it by their own courage and enthusiasm in whatever role the future may demand of them. This standard, which has now received God's blessing, we will cherish in peace and in war."

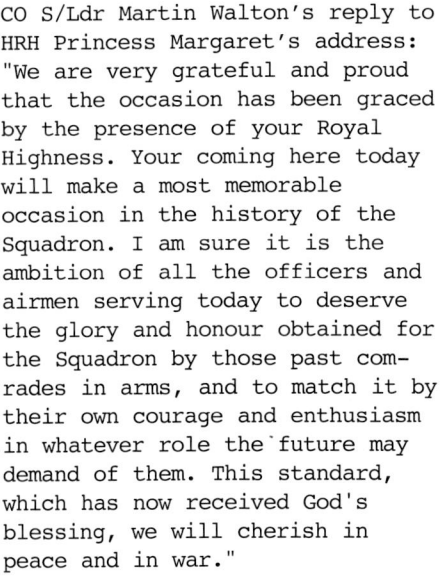 

Squadron Inspection by HRH Princess Margaret (F/Lt David Waite with sword).

CO S/Ldr Martin Walton bidding farewell to HRH Princess Margaret, as 605 Hon A/Cdr Alan Cecil Wright AFC TD looks on.

15 August 1954: C/O S/Ldr Martin Walton makes the news.

1954: Honiley Control Tower. The safety of 605's pilots was always in the excellent and highly-trained hands of Senior Air Traffic Controller F/Lt John Fox and his superb team.

1954: F/Lt David Waite looks on as a number of Vampire FB.5s are refuelled on the line.

1954: Standing: Gordon Lee & Billy Dees. Sitting: Stan Hartland, Claude Chambers & Brian Gopsill at Thornaby

1954: C/O S/Ldr Martin Walton briefing some 605 pilots at Honiley. Back row: Jerry Edgerton, Tubby Homer, Ray Raby & David Waite. Front row: Allen Whitworth DFC, Don Sergeant & John Towle.

1954: F/Lt David Waite puts Vampire FB.5 WA360(H) through it's paces

The two occupants of this Meteor jet trainer walked clear after it had crash-landed in a ploughed field near Baginton aerodrome, Coventry, yesterday. The machine was on a training flight from Honiley.

PILOTS OF CRASHED METEOR UNINJURED

TWO Warwickshire pilots of No. 605 Squadron, Royal Auxiliary Air Force, escaped without injury when they made a crash landing in a Meteor jet trainer in a ploughed field near Baginton Aerodrome, Coventry, yesterday.

The machine, which was based at Honiley, broke through a hedge and came to rest in the field on the Leamington Road side of the aerodrome after the pilot, Flight-Lieutenant D. P. Shepherd, had tried to make a glide approach into Baginton. The co-pilot was Flight-Officer J. Edgerton.

A guard was mounted near the 'plane and arrangements made to move it back to Honiley. The cause of the crash is not yet known, but an investigation will follow.

HARD DAY FOR PILOTS AND GROUND CREWS

Air-firing Exercises Delayed by Mist

From Our Air Correspondent

GIBRALTAR, Wednesday

The evening sun was bathing the Rock with a reddish golden glow as 605 (County of Warwick) Squadron Vampires from Honiley touched down on the North Front runway for the last time to-day.

It has been a hard day for pilots and particularly for ground crews, who have been working since 7.30 a.m.

The pressure on the squadron to get off as many air-firing exercises as possible in a comparatively short time has been due to the peculiar mist which has caused flying to be cancelled every morning since we arrived.

The ground crews have taken advantage of the "no flying" weather to inspect the aircraft thoroughly. Their standard of maintenance has been highly praised.

One ground crew number, A.C. Alex McKenzie, from Coventry, has gained a reputation for keenness by diving into the sea to rescue flag targets. A lost target means that pilots who have fired at them would have to do that particular exercise again, so A.C. McKenzie's zeal is looked upon with great favour by those pilots who have reason to believe they have made good scores.

Crowded Programme

A normal day's flying programme has had to be crowded into a single afternoon to-day, and weather forecasts threaten a similar cramming to-morrow. The ground mist, caused by warm winds from the east striking the comparatively cool Rock, is expected again to-morrow.

This morning, with the mist cloying the runway, it was still possible to sunbathe, since on the Spanish frontier side of the aerodrome the air was perfectly clear.

The squadron will be giving up its free day on Saturday to take a major part in Gibraltar's first Battle of Britain air display for at least three years. The display will not start until the afternoon, but the Vampire fighters will probably be on airfiring exercises throughout the morning as well.

When the squadron returns to Honiley in about a week's time there will still be a few days of its annual 15 days' training left. These will be spent in a highly concentrated flying programme from its home aerodrome. The pilots will be taking part in a major fighter exercise at this time.

Footnote: A 605 Auxiliary football team beat a Gibraltar R.A.F. Station team by 2-1 to-day.

1955: John Towle, Jerry Edgerton & Murray Smalley

1955: 605 ground crew working on Vampire FB.5 WA291 in the sun.

FAST FLIGHT TO GIB. BY 605 SQUADRON

People in Gibraltar have already been impressed by 605 (County of Warwick) Squadron from Honiley, which is training for 12 days at Gibraltar. Ten Vampire jet aircraft made a more than 1,000-mile formation flight from Tangmere to Gibraltar in about three-and-a-half hours.

Although the squadron is not claiming this as a record, it is regarded as the fastest flight any Royal Auxiliary Air Force squadron has made from England.

The aircraft made one stop for refuelling at an aerodrome near Marseilles, then flew over Spain after special permission had been given, arriving over Gibraltar's north front aerodrome in two formations —one of six and one of four aircraft.

They flew twice round the Rock—which is in the middle of the aerodrome's flying circuit—before landing in quick succession. So many aircraft landing in so short a time was a rarity here, I was told. The road into Spain runs across the runway and bus loads of passengers held up by the fighters, watched a free and unexpected display with delight.

Seconds after the aircraft engines had stopped, ground crews, who had arrived earlier in three Hastings transport aircraft, were stripping the Vampires down in the hot sun and preparing them for operational fitness.

The flight from England had been made at about 30,000 feet with long range tanks fitted to the wings. The leading formation was led by the officer commanding the squadron, Sq.-Ldr. P. M. R. Walton.

AIR DISPLAY

In addition to the squadron's training it will take a major part in what will be Gibraltar's first Battle of Britain air display for at least three years. Squadron pilots will give aerobatics and formation flying displays. With their reputation already made good here by their first fast flight from England, they have been made conscious that people are looking forward to the air show now with even greater enthusiasm than before the squadron's arrival.

Flying training began yesterday under the imposing bulk of "The Rock," and ground crews worked hard to get the aircraft away and into the air so that pilots could assess flying conditions. These "familiarisation flights" are very necessary, since the aerodrome runway is one of the most peculiar in the world, on which to take-off and land. There are usually winds blowing from three different directions at once over the landing strip; winds at each end being in direct opposition. Relaxation from flying and maintenance duties came in the evening when most of the squadron personnel visited the local town, finding it a gay and entertaining place.

During the off-duty periods in the daytime many members of the squadron have been going to Mediterranean beaches. Plans for future evenings have been made for trips into Spain, particularly to see much advertised bull fights. Even short visit visas have been difficult to obtain, however, and so far usually only those who arranged for visas in England have been able to organise a trip across the border.

Summer 1956: 605 enjoying a beer in the Gibraltar Yacht Club, in what was to be the Squadron's last Summer Camp.

Gibraltar 1956: 605 flexing it's muscles!

1956: An every day scene at Honiley, refuelling Vampire FB.5 WA360(M)

Late 1950s: Officers Mess at Honiley. L-R: Harry Matty, David Waite, John Towle, CO Martin Walton, Tubby Homer, ?, Jerry Edgerton, Johnny Walker and Don Sergeant

1956: Formation of Vampire FB.5s: WA360(H), VZ870(E), WG807(M), VV520(D), WA456(C) & VZ307(A)

1956: A formation of Vampire FB.5s prepare to take to the Warwickshire skies

11 Jan 1957: A lone 605 Vampire FB.5 taxis across the Honiley tarmac for the last time. The last sortie was flown by Jerry Edgerton, who poignantly wrote in his log-book "LAST AUX PILOT TO FLY ON 605". After 31 years as an operational Squadron; 605 was formally disbanded on 11 March 1957.

605 – THE LEGEND LIVES ON

1990: 605 Squadron Memorial and Rose Garden; St Cuthbert's Church, Castle Vale, Birmingham. 605 will be forever indebted to our Honorary Architect David Adams for his magnificent efforts in ensuring that 605 has a memorial to be very proud of. St Cuthbert's is located on the old airfield at Castle Bromwich.

Midland Air Museum, Coventry Airport, Warwickshire

de Havilland Vampire F.1 VF301 (RAL-G) resplendent in 605 Squadron markings. The Vampire is the superb centrepiece of the excellent 605 section at the Midland Air Museum at Coventry Airport. 605 were based at RAF Baginton (as it was once known) in 1941, and have since formed a very close relationship with the museum, who have become the official custodians of all our Squadron memorabilia. The museum is constantly on the lookout for any additional 605 material for their display. If you do have any items you would like to donate to the Museum, then please contact Barry or Diane James on 02476 301033 or email them on: midlandairmuseum@aol.com

Part of the collection of 605 Squadron Silver held at the Town Hall, Stratford-upon-Avon. L-R: Silver Mosquito presented to 605 by Hon. Air Commodore Sir Lindsay Everard M.P. to commemorate the 100th enemy aircraft destroyed by 605 in Jan 44 (see page 52). Silver Bear and Ragged Staff presented by Hon. Air Commodore Lord Bearsted M.C. "in recognition of seven happy years" as our Hon. A/Cdr. Silver Hawker Hart K3886, and Silver Hurricane presented to 605 by the Directors of Hawker Aircraft and Rolls Royce Ltd in 1940.

ROLL OF HONOUR

LAC Leonard Francis ABBOTT, Age 22	27 Aug 1939 (1)
Sgt Charles Corringham ADAMS, Pilot, Age 21	21 May 1943
F/Sgt Richard George ALDWORTH, Pilot, Age 20	11 Jan 1944
F/Lt George ALLEN, Pilot, Age 20	2 Feb 1942
LAC Brian Charles AMBLER, Age 22	14 Jun 1942 *
F/Lt John Norman ANDREWS, Pilot	26 Sep 1944
LAC William ANZANI	24 Jan 1944 *
F/O Albert Victor AYLOTT, Pilot	3 Aug 1943
F/O W.Colin BARNABY, Pilot	9 Dec 1934
F/Lt John Rogers BECKETT (R.A.A.F.), Pilot, Age 27	23 Mar 1944
LAC Eric BELFIELD, Age 19	22 Apr 1943 *
P/O Ronald Jeffrey BENNETT, Pilot, Age 24	20 Jul 1942
F/Lt Basil Godfrey BENSTED, Pilot	2 Oct 1944
AC1 Arthur Henry BERESFORD	24 Jun 1944 *
F/Lt Frank BERESFORD, Nav, Age 28	11 Apr 1945
S/Ldr Ian Maxwell Theodore de BOCOCK, Pilot, Age 32	24 Apr 1943
F/Sgt Ronald Arthur BOND, Nav, Age 21	25 May 1944
F/Lt Victor George BREWIS, Nav, Age 28	6 Jun 1944
F/O Robert Oliver BRIGDEN, Pilot, Age 21	1 Sep 1944
LAC Jack Alfred BROADMORE, Age 24	14 Feb 1942 *
Sgt Robert BROWN, Nav, Age 22	24 Apr 1943
AC2 Victor Lewis Clarke BROWN, Age 23	29 Nov 1943 *
F/Sgt Graham Herbert BRYAN, Age 29	21 Jul 1943 *
F/O Raymond Paul BULMAN, Pilot, Age 21	9 Feb 1945
LAC Stanley Percy BURGE, Age 24	11 Oct 1944 *
P/O Cyril Lawrence BURRAGE, Nav	2 Oct 1944
LAC S. R. Butcher	1 Dec 1942 *
LAC Jack BUZAN, Age 22	1 May 1942 *
LAC Ian Ross CARMICHAEL, Age 32	18 Sep 1944 *
AC1 Ernest Edward CHECKETTS, Age 21	29 Nov 1943 *
F/Sgt Albert CHILTON, Nav, Age 21	26 May 1943
W/O Henry John COLLINS, Pilot, Age 22	3 Aug 1945
P/O Eric Arthur COOMBES, Age 35	20 Sep 1942
F/Lt Arnold John CRAVEN D.F.C., Pilot, Age 27	31 Oct 1944
AC1 Arthur Albert CROFTS	6 Oct 1943 *
F/O Peter Guerin CROFTS, Pilot, Age 22	28 Sep 1940
F/O Kenneth Fraser DACRE D.F.C., Pilot	22 Sep 1943
F/O Peter John DANIELSEN, Pilot, Age 26	17 May 1940
AC2 Joyda Howell DAVIES, Age 22	23 Jul 1943 *
Sgt Sidney Rowland DIDSBURY D.F.M., Nav, Age 31	22 Sep 1943
Sgt Kenneth Lindsay DODDS, Age 24	16 Nov 1944 *
AC1 Colin Frederick DOUGLAS	25 Nov 1942 *
LAC Fred Charles DOWDING	12 Dec 1942 *
P/O K. DUNIN, Pilot	18 Mar 1945
P/O Thomas Anthony DUNPHY, Nav, Age 20	30 Aug 1942
Cpl Wilfrid Brazier DURK, Age 25	1 Dec 1942 *
AC1 Colin Stuart EARL, Age 43	29 Nov 1943 *
F/O Ernest James EDWARDS, Age 21	22 Feb 1944
P/O Charles Edward ENGLISH, Pilot, Age 28	7 Oct 1940
F/Lt Jack George ENTICOTT, Pilot, Age 25	22 Feb 1945

F/O Percival James Samuel EVANS, Nav	3 Aug 1943
LAC Wilfred Campbell Lloyd EVANS, Age 30	6 Oct 1944 *
AC2 Maxwell FOAN, Age 22	24 Jun 1944 *
P/O George Mathwin FORRESTER, Pilot, Age 26	9 Sep 1940
AC1 Ronald FOSTER	13 Jun 1944 (2)
F/Lt John FOTHERINGHAM-PARKER, Pilot, Age 31	25 May 1944
P/O Patrick Constable FRASER, Pilot, Age 20	12 Dec 1939
Sgt Wilfred FREEMAN, Nav, Age 21	26 Sep 1944
Sgt James Frederick FRY, Nav, Age 22	9 Mar 1945
F/O Arthur Jack GAPPER, Age 28	7 Apr 1944
F/Lt Denys Henson Hugh GATHERCOLE D.F.C., Pilot, Age 24	8 Jun 1944
P/O C. GAUZE, Pilot	15 Nov 1940
AC1 Ronald Joseph GIBBS	3 Dec 1942 *
F/O Colin Cuthill GIBSON (R.A.A.F.), Age 30	18 Jan 1945
AC1 William GIBSON, Age 28	26 Dec 1942 *
LAC Arthur Ernest GILES	25 Aug 1942 *
P/O Witold Jozef GLOWACKI V.M. (Poland), Pilot	24 Sep 1940
P/O Barrie Laughton GOODWIN, Pilot, Age 23	24 Jun 1940
AC1 Henry Nicholas GREEVES, Age 36	3 May 1945 *
AC1 Ronald GREENWOOD	8 Sep 1943 *
AC1 Frank Herbert HALL, Age 32	14 Feb 1942 *
AC1 John Isaac Thomas HANCOCK, Age 30	18 Sep 1944 *
AC1 Thomas HARPER, Age 25	12 Aug 1943 *
AC1 Alfred Frank HARRIS	29 Nov 1943 *
LAC John HARRIS	19 Nov 1942 *
Cpl Henry William HARRODINE, Age 27	26 Mar 1942 *
Cpl Jack HART	1 Oct 1943 *
F/Lt Stanley Harry HATSELL D.F.C., Nav, Age 23	17 Mar 1945
P/O Graham O. HAUSER, Pilot	28 Nov 1955
F/Lt Glen Allen HOLLAND (R.C.A.F.), Pilot	21 Apr 1944
F/O Ralph HOPE, Pilot, Age 27	14 Oct 1940
Cpl Edmund HORLER, Age 22	17 Feb 1944 *
F/O Albert Alexander HORVATH, Pilot, Age 25	5 Nov 1942
Sgt Harold Norman HOWES D.F.M., Pilot, Age 24	22 Dec 1940
S/Ldr Jack David HUMPHREYS D.F.C., Pilot	2 Aug 1942
AC1 Walter HUTCHINSON, Age 35	12 Oct 1942 *
F/Lt Gerald O'Farrel Grant HYNE, Pilot	26 Nov 1943
W/O Albert Dennis JACK	19 Jul 1944
Cpl Harold Vincent JAMES, Age 34	14 Feb 1942 *
F/Lt Edward Leonard JONES, Pilot, Age 25	22 Feb 1945
P/O Geoffrey MacFarlane JORDAN, Age 19	30 Aug 1942
Cpl William KELLY, Age 21	15 Feb 1942 *
Cpl A. KEMP	25 Jun 1942 *
F/Sgt S. KEMP, Age 25	29 Nov 1943 *
Sgt Oldrich KESTLER (Czechoslovakia), Pilot, Age 28	7 Apr 1941
F/Sgt Norman James LEES, Nav, Age 20	27 Sep 1944
LAC Harold Leonard LEWIS, Age 26	21 Jan 1944 *
AC1 Leonard Ernest LEYBURN, Age 26	13 Jun 1944 (2)
AC1 Cecil Frank LOVE, Age 38	29 Nov 1943 *
P/O Peter William LOWE, Pilot, Age 19	15 Feb 1942
F/O Graham Murray LUMSDEN (R.A.A.F.), Pilot, Age 26	18 Jan 1945
Sgt Robert Marwick MAINLAND, Pilot	25 Apr 1940

W/O Douglas Leslie McCONNEL, Nav, Age 27	2 Aug 1942
F/Sgt John Finlay McEWEN (R.C.A.F.), Nav	22 Oct 1943
Sgt Peter Roy Charles McINTOSH, Pilot, Age 20	12 Oct 1940
S/Ldr Archibald Ashmore McKELLAR D.S.O. D.F.C. & Bar, Pilot, Age 28	1 Nov 1940
LAC John McLAUGHLIN, Age 24	26 Sep 1944 *
F/Lt Andrew Crawford Rankin McLURE, Pilot, Age 24	20 Jul 1942
W/Cdr Richard Angelo MITCHELL D.F.C. & Bar, Pilot, Age 35	17 Mar 1945
Sgt MOFFAT, Pilot	22 May 1940
F/Lt Ian James MUIRHEAD D.F.C., Pilot, Age 27	15 Oct 1940
P/O Kevin Joseph MULCAIR (R.C.A.F.), Nav, Age 21	11 Jan 1944
Cpl Donald Carden NEIL, Age 30	11 Sep 1943 *
S/Ldr Michael NEGUS D.F.C., Pilot	7 Apr 1944
AC1 Ernest William NELSON, Age 26	10 Dec 1942 *
F/Lt William Gerald OLDHAM (R.C.A.F.), Pilot	9 Mar 1945
F/Lt Michael George OLLEY A.F.C., Pilot, Age 25	10 Mar 1943
F/O Robert James Rex OWEN, Pilot, Age 21	22 Feb 1945
Cpl John Eden PALMER	29 Nov 1943 *
Sgt Ivor Glynn PARRY, Age 45	8 Dec 1942 *
LAC Edward PARSONS, Age 23	22 Dec 1943 *
LAC Alfred Arthur PERKS, Age 22	14 Feb 1942 *
S/Ldr George Vivian PERRY, Pilot	27 May 1940
Sgt Henry William PETTIT, Pilot, Age 20	2 Feb 1941
F/O Gerwyn PHILLIPS, Nav	22 Feb 1945
P/O Roy Edgar PHILLIPS, Nav, Age 21	26 Jun 1944
F/Lt Richard Carrington PICKERING, Pilot, Age 23	22 Feb 1944
P/O Kenneth James PIERPOINT, Pilot, Age 20	28 Aug 1942
LAC Alfred Leslie Frank PONT, Age 30	29 Nov 1943 *
Sgt William Thomas POULSON	1 Dec 1942 *
AC1 Charles Gilbert PUGH	24 Jun 1944 *
F/O Kenneth Henry RAY, Nav, Age 23	11 May 1944
F/Lt John REID DFM, Pilot, Age 23	26 Jun 1944
LAC Henry James REYNOLDS	14 Jun 1943 *
Sgt Robert Douglas RITCHIE, Pilot, Age 24	9 Aug 1940
AC1 Arthur David ROBINSON	13 Dec 1942 *
F/O Ian Cedric ROGERSON (R.N.Z.A.F.), Nav, Age 24	9 Nov 1944
Sgt Norman Edward Albert ROSS, Pilot	21 Oct 1942
P/O John Hedley ROTHWELL, Pilot, Age 20	22 Feb 1941
LAC Arthur Frederick RUSSON, Age 22	1 Dec 1942 *
P/O Alec Maxtone Wright SCOTT, Pilot, Age 29	2 Jan 1941
Cpl Edwards SCOTT, Age 23	13 Dec 1942 *
AC1 Derrick William SHOULER, Age 23	29 Nov 1943 *
F/Lt Richard Maitland SINGER (R.N.Z.A.F.), Pilot, Age 23	9 Nov 1944
F/Sgt Eric Granville Moreton SMITH, Pilot, Age 23	26 May 1943
F/Lt Leslie Alexander William SMITH, Age 21	19 Mar 1945
Sgt Robert Jean-Baptiste Edmond STENUIT (Belgium), Pilot	22 Oct 1943
Cpl Joseph STEVENS, Age 21	1 Dec 1942 *
Sgt James Crawford STIRRAT, W.Op/AG, Age 28	31 Dec 1942
F/Lt John Lister STORER, Pilot, Age 22	27 Sep 1944
LAC Ronald Ernest TABER, Age 21	25 Jul 1942 *
LAC John Norman TASKER, Age 24	14 Jun 1943 *
AC2 Harry John TAYLOR	1 Apr 1940
P/O George THIRWELL, Nav, Age 22	22 Feb 1945

AC2 Hilton Lloyd THOMAS, Age 26	4 Dec 1942 *
F/O Frank THOMPSON, Nav, Age 21	27 Mar 1945
LAC Ronald Henry Curtis TINDLE	8 Apr 1945 *
LAC Cyril Geoffrey TOOTH, Age 28	29 Nov 1943 *
F/O Frederick Dutton TOPPING, Nav	23 Mar 1944
LAC Roy Eastwood TOWNLEY, Age 21	13 Jun 1944 (2)
F/Lt John Robert TRACEY, Pilot, Age 27	11 Apr 1945
F/O Anthony Noel Hailes TUSTAIN, Pilot, Age 20	20 Jul 1942
F/O William Martin Ross Reid URQUHART, Pilot, Age 23	27 Jul 1943
Sgt Robert VEITCH, Nav, Age 27	31 Dec 1942
W/O Harry VIPOND D.F.C., Nav, Age 26	10 Mar 1943
Sgt Charles Harry WALDER, Pilot, Age 23	26 Nov 1943
Cpl Alfred William WARD, Age 32	25 Aug 1944 *
F/O Douglas Frederick WARREN, Nav, Age 35	9 Feb 1945
F/O John Henry WARREN, Pilot	19 Sep 1939
Sgt James WARRENDER, Pilot, Age 27	31 Dec 1942
F/O Adam Gardener McArthur WATSON, Nav, Age 22	27 Jul 1943
Sgt William Ralph WELLS, W.Op/AG	2 Aug 1942
W/O Albert Henry WETTONE, Nav, Age 23	8 Jun 1944
LAC William Henry Herbert WHITFIELD, Age 20	3 Dec 1942 *
F/Lt Arthur WHITTEN-BROWN, Pilot	6 Jun 1944
F/O Roger Howard WILKINSON, Nav, Age 21	21 Apr 1944
F/O Raymond William WILSON, Pilot, Age 24	27 Mar 1945
LAC Robert WOOD, Age 27	2 Nov 1944 *
F/Sgt Leonard William WOODARD D.F.M., Nav	31 Oct 1944
F/Lt Trevor Laurance McAlpine WOODS, Pilot, Age 28	11 May 1944
F/Sgt William George WOOLDRIDGE, Age 34	24 Jun 1944
Sgt Eddie WRIGHT, Nav, Age 22	21 May 1943
F/O Gilbert Francis Moncreiff WRIGHT, Pilot, Age 36	22 May 1940
F/O Harold Lewis WRIGHT, Pilot, Age 33	14 Feb 1942
AC1 John Hally YORK	8 Apr 1942 *

* Denotes killed in action by the Japanese in 1942, or captured and died as a Prisoner Of War.

(1) LAC Leonard Francis Abbott was killed 27/8/1939 whilst driving a Fordson Tractor unit from Castle Bromwich to Tangmere. He swerved to avoid some children playing in the ford at Kenilworth and was killed when the unit fell down an embankment.

(2) AC1 Ronald Foster, AC1 Leonard Ernest Leyburn & LAC Roy Eastwood Townley were killed 13/6/1944 at Manston when one 500lb and eight 20lb bombs exploded whilst they were rearming a Squadron Mosquito. The cause was never established, but it was deemed very unlikely that any of the three experienced armourers were at fault.

COMMANDING OFFICERS

S/Ldr J.A.C. Wright A.F.C. T.D.	Oct 1926
S/Ldr Lord Willoughby de Broke M.C. A.F.C.	Mar 1936
S/Ldr G.V. Perry	Dec 1939
F/Lt R.F. Grant-Ferris M.P.	May 1940 *
S/Ldr W.M. Churchill D.S.O. D.F.C.	Jun 1940
S/Ldr A.A. McKellar D.F.C.	Sep 1940
F/Lt C.F. Currant D.F.C.	Nov 1940 *
S/Ldr G.R. Edge D.F.C.	Nov 1940
S/Ldr R. Reid	Sep 1941
S/Ldr S.E. Andrews D.F.M.	Jan 1942
S/Ldr E.W. Wright D.F.C.	Feb 1942
W/Cdr P.W. Townsend D.S.O. D.F.C.	Jun 1942
W/Cdr G.L. Denholm D.F.C.	Aug 1942
W/Cdr C.D. Tomalin A.F.C.	May 1943
W/Cdr B.R.O'B. Hoare D.S.O. D.F.C. and Bar	Sep 1943
W/Cdr N.J. Starr D.F.C.	Apr 1944
W/Cdr R.A. Mitchell D.F.C. & Bar	Sep 1944
S/Ldr A.G. Woods D.F.C.	Mar 1945 *
W/Cdr A.W. Horne D.F.C. A.F.C.	Apr 1945
S/Ldr I.F. McCall D.F.C.	Jul 1945 *
S/Ldr R.J. Walker D.S.O.	May 1946
S/Ldr R.C.T. Goodwin	Dec 1947
S/Ldr J.A. Timmis	Jul 1949
S/Ldr P.M.R. Walton	Aug 1951
S/Ldr R.E. Tickner	May 1956

* Acting Commanding Officer

BASES

RAF Castle Bromwich, Warwickshire	5 Oct 1926 - 27 Aug 1939
RAF Tangmere, Sussex	27 Aug 1939 - 11 Feb 1940
RAF Leuchars, Fife	11 Feb 1940 - 27 Feb 1940
RAF Wick, Caithness	27 Feb 1940 - 21 May 1940
RAF Hawkinge, Kent	21 May 1940 - 28 May 1940
RAF Drem, Lothian	28 May 1940 - 7 Sep 1940
RAF Croydon, Surrey	7 Sep 1940 - 26 Feb 1941
RAF Martlesham Heath, Suffolk	26 Feb 1941 - 31 Mar 1941
RAF Ternhill, Shropshire	31 Mar 1941 - 1 Jul 1941
RAF Baginton, Warwickshire	1 Jul 1941 - 4 Sep 1941
RAF Honiley, Warwickshire	4 Sep 1941 - Dec 1941
RAF Hal Far, Malta (1)	12 Nov 1941 - 27 Feb 1942
Batavia, Java	3 Feb 1942 - 10 Feb 1942
Palembang, Sumatra (2)	10 Feb 1942 - 14 Feb 1942
RAF Ford, Sussex (3)	7 Jun 1942 - 15 Mar 1943
RAF Castle Camps, Cambridgeshire	15 Mar 1943 - 6 Oct 1943
RAF Bradwell Bay, Essex	6 Oct 1943 - 7 Apr 1944
RAF Manston, Kent	7 Apr 1944 - 21 Nov 1944
RAF Hartford Bridge, Hampshire	21 Nov 1944 - 15 Mar 1945
Coxyde (B.71), Belgium	15 Mar 1945 - 28 Apr 1945
Volkel (B.80), Holland (4)	28 Apr 1945 - 31 Aug 1945
RAF Honiley, Warwickshire (5)(6)	10 May 1946 - 11 Mar 1957

(1) Disbanded 27 Feb 1942, 605 personnel joined No.185 Squadron.
(2) Disbanded 14 Feb 1942, 605 personnel joined forces with Nos.238 and 242 Squadrons.
(3) Reformed 7 Jun 1942.
(4) Disbanded 31 Aug 1945 and renumbered No.4 Squadron
(5) Reformed as an Auxiliary Squadron 10 May 1946.
(6) Disbanded 11 Mar 1957.

HONOURS & AWARDS

Bar to the Distinguished Service Order

W/Cdr B.R.O'B. Hoare D.S.O. D.F.C. & Bar	Apr 1944

Distinguished Service Order

S/Ldr A.A. McKellar D.F.C.	Nov 1940

Bar to the Distinguished Flying Cross

P/O C.F. Currant D.F.C.	Nov 1940
F/Lt C.E. Knowles D.F.C.	Mar 1944
F/Lt A.D. Wagner D.F.C.	Apr 1944
W/Cdr R.A. Mitchell D.F.C.	Jul 1944
F/O F.E. Hogg D.F.C.	Jul 1944
W/Cdr N.J. Starr D.F.C.	Nov 1944
S/Ldr L.H.W. Welch D.F.C.	Jan 1945
S/Ldr A.G. Woods D.F.C.	Oct 1945

Distinguished Flying Cross

P/O I.J. Muirhead	Jun 1940
F/Lt A.A. McKellar	Sep 1940
S/Ldr G.R. Edge	Sep 1940
P/O C.F. Currant	Oct 1940
F/O P.L. Parrott	Oct 1940
F/O T.P.M. Cooper-Slipper	Nov 1940
F/Lt J.E.M. Williams	Nov 1942
F/Lt H.M. Maggs	Mar 1943
F/O P.D.J. Wood	Jul 1943
F/O R.R. Smart	Jul 1943
S/Ldr A.W. Mack	Sep 1943
F/O K.F. Dacre	Oct 1943
F/Lt D.H. Blomeley	Oct 1943
W/Cdr C.D. Tomalin A.F.C.	Oct 1943
F/O A.G. Woods	Mar 1944
F/O E.L. Williams	Apr 1944
F/O E.T. Orringe	Apr 1944
F/O R.C. Muir	Apr 1944

S/Ldr M. Negus	Apr 1944
F/Lt L.H. Hodder	May 1944
F/Lt W.A. Bird	Jun 1944
F/O S.H. Hatsell	Sep 1944
P/O J. Irvine	Sep 1944
F/Lt R. Birrell	Nov 1944
S/Ldr K.M. Carver	Nov 1944
F/Lt A.J. Craven	Jan 1945
F/O R.E. Lelong	Jan 1945
P/O A.J. McLaren	Jan 1945
S/Ldr J.I. Pengelly	Apr 1945
F/O A.T. Linn	Jun 1945
W/O W. Harrison D.F.M.	Jun 1945
F/Lt B. Williams	Jul 1945
W/O S.E. Hardy	Jul 1945
F/Lt C.F. Ponsford	Sep 1945
F/Lt J.C. Worthington	Sep 1945
F/O F.A. Friar	Sep 1945
S/Ldr I.F. McCall	Sep 1945
F/Lt G. Robertson	Oct 1945
F/O W.H. Johnson D.F.M.	Oct 1945
P/O A.E. Gregory	Unknown
S/Ldr T.A. Heath A.F.C. & Bar	Unknown
W/O H. Vipond	Unknown

Air Force Cross

F/Lt M.G. Olley	Feb 1943

Distinguished Flying Medal

Sgt H.N. Howes	Oct 1940
Sgt E.W. Wright	Nov 1940
Sgt S.R. Didsbury	Oct 1943
F/Sgt W.H. Johnson	Mar 1944
F/Sgt L.W. Woodard	Jan 1945

Member of the Order of the British Empire

F/Lt A.C. Dunn
F/Lt D.J.N. Rebbeck

British Empire Medal

F/Sgt R.P.H. Gibbs

Mention in Despatches

F/Lt A.M. Michie
F/O J.K. Sutcliffe
F/Sgt G. Ritchie
LAC J.J. Smith
P/O D.H. Wiseman
P/O E.J. House
Sgt R.C. Martin
Sgt W.A. Winpenny
W/O J.W. Tredwen
Sgt J.D. Hanson
W/O H.J. Collins
W/Cdr B.R.O'B. Hoare D.S.O. & Bar D.F.C. & Bar

SQUADRON AIRCRAFT

Avro 504K: Oct 1926
E9543; F9828; H2402

Avro 504N: Oct 1926
J8510; J8686; J8689; J8711; J8768; J8772; K1806; K1968; K1987; K2364; K2387

Handley Page DH9A: Oct 1926
E8656; E8686; E8711; J7814; J7836; J8107; J8109; J8125; J8162; J8163; J8225; J8480

Westland Wapiti IIA: Apr 1930
J9651; J9837; J9861; J9864; J9865; J9866; J9868; K1136; K1141; K1145; K1146; K1147; K1148; K1155; K1156; K1157; K1342; K1343; K1367; K1368; K1370; K1376; K1377; K2237; K2238

DeHavilland DH60 Tiger Moth: Early 1930's
K1206; K1216; L9630

Hawker Hart: Oct 1934
K1423; K2435; K2439; K2452; K2458; K2459; K2461; K2462; K2465; K2467; K2989; K3010; K3017; K3018; K3032; K3051; K3756; K3768; K3790; K3857; K3861; K3877; K3883; K3885; K3886; K3887; K3888; K3889; K3890; K3891; K3892

Hawker Hind: Aug 1936
K5431; K5467; K5514; K5531; K5532; K5533; K5534; K5535; K5536; K5537; K5538; K5539; K5540; K5541; K6672; K6674; K6676; K6726; L7237

Avro Tutor: 1937
K3309; K3311; K3457; K3458; K3459

Fairey Battle: 1937
N2108; N2109

Gloster Gladiator I: Apr 1939
K6145; K7917; K7942 (HE-H); K7946 (HE-R); K7952; K7961; K7965; K7979; K7985; K8004; K8032; K8044

Gloster Gladiator II: Apr 1939
N2303; N2304; N2305; N2306; N2308; N2309; N2310; N2311; N2312 (HE-O); N2313; N2314; N5576; N5577; N5578; N5580; N5581; N5583 (HE-Q); N5585 (HE-R); N5586 (HE-K)

Hawker Hurricane I: Aug 1939
L1830; L2012; L2012; L2013; L2014 (UP-U); L2018; L2020; L2021; L2022 (UP-L); L2058; L2059; L2061; L2101; L2103; L2103; L2118; L2119; L2120; L2121; L2122 (UP-L); L3575; N2346; N2349; N2352 (UP-N); N2546; N2557; P2560; P2717 (UP-O); P2765 (UP-N); P2916; P2994; P3022 (UP-M); P3107 (UP-O); P3423; P3580; P3581; P3583; P3588; P3650 (UP-D); P3677; P3737; P3827; P3828 (UP-R); P3832; P3965 (UP-P); V6699; V6755 (UP-L); V6783; V6786; V6844; V6879; V6951; V7305; V7599 (UP-U); V7609

Hawker Hurricane II: Dec 1940
Z2308; Z2323; Z2329; Z2347

Douglas Boston III: Jun 1942

DeHavilland Mosquito NF.II: Feb 1943
DZ691; DZ714; DZ716 (UP-L); DZ717; DZ723; DZ724 (UP-S);

DeHavilland Mosquito FB.VI: Jun 1943
HJ761 (UP-P); HJ766; HJ767 (UP-G); HJ768 (UP-Q);
HJ775 (UP-U); HJ776 (UP-E); HJ778 (UP-A); HJ779 (UP-L);
HJ780 (UP-X); HJ785 (UP-T); HJ808 (UP-O); HJ827 (UP-K);
HR152 (UP-S); HR203 (UP-V); HR205 (UP-A); HR206 (UP-M);
HR349 (UP-W); HR363 (UP-U); MM414 (UP-Y); MM429 (UP-H);
NS838 (UP-J); NS876 (UP-P); NS880 (UP-M); NS914 (UP-X);
PZ349 (UP-A); PZ381 (UP-K); RS567 (UP-S); RS678 (UP-T);
SZ967 (UP-U); SZ993 (UP-A); TA112 (UP-O); TA117 (UP-Y);
TA383 (UP-Y)

DeHavilland Mosquito NF.36: Apr 1947
NT301; NT325; TA307 (V)

DeHavilland Vampire F.1: Apr 1948
TG349; TG381 (RAL-A); TG384; TG424 (NR-G); TG427 (NR-H);
VF279

Harvard: Apr 1948
KF180;

DeHavilland Vampire FB.5: Jun 1951
VV520; VV529 (D); VZ307 (A); VZ336 (L); VZ870 (E); WA291;
WA329 (NR-G); WA360 (H)&(C); WA364; WA456 (C); WG807 (M)

Gloster Meteor T7
WA734

SQUADRON AIRCRAFT IDENTIFICATION CODES
HE   Apr 1939 - Sep 1939
UP   Sep 1939 - Aug 1945
RAL   May 1946 - Jun 1950
NR   Jun 1950 - Aug 1951

ADDITIONAL READING
"We Never Slept, The Story of 605 Squadron" by Ian Piper
264 pages, 24 illustrations.
ISBN No: 0 9529516 0 6

ACKNOWLEDGEMENTS
This book would not of been possible without the invaluable support from a large number of people. Richard Pember and Arif Sheikh deserve a special mention. Richard was responsible for the superb book cover and the formatting and artwork throughout the book. Arif was responsible for the excellent 605 website www.605squadron.com. I am especially indebted to James and Andrew Churchill, son and grandson of the late W/Cdr Walter Churchill D.S.O. D.F.C.

605 Squadron
W/Cdr Graham Austin O.B.E. A.F.C. A.E., Basil Cherverton
Ernie Currill, G/Cpt Gerry Edge O.B.E. D.F.C. A.E.
Ken Filby, Peter Freeman-Pannett A.E.,George Furley
William Gibbon, Reg Jones, Terrence "Flash" Kelly
F/Lt Hugh Louden, W/Cdr Maynard "Mitch" Mitchell D.F.C. A.E.
S/Ldr Bob Muir D.F.C., Joan Peace, Grev Redford
Terry Short, Cherry Symonds W.A.A.F.
S/Ldr Arthur Woods D.F.C.

605 Squadron - Association Committee
F/Lt Peter Rudd D.F.C. A.E. (President)
Arthur "Soapy" Hudson A.E. (Chairman)
Geoff Greenwood A.E. (Secretary)
David Adams (Hon. Architect)
Pat Chapman, Norman Connew A.E., Frank Henderson
Ray Hinsley, Gordon Lee, Harry "Butch" Lloyd A.E.,
Eddie Oakley, Colin Sawrey, Bill Sunburk A.E.,
Des Timmins A.E., John Walsh, Bob Webb

JJ Churchill Ltd, Market Bosworth, Leics
James Churchill; Andrew Churchill

Hilton Birmingham Metropole Hotel, NEC, Birmingham
The management and staff, past and present, for their unwavering support for 605 over the last 13 years.

Midland Air Museum, Baginton, Warwickshire
Barry James, Diane James

Louis Drapkin (Printers)
David Herbert

My two wonderful daughters, Hannah & Sophie

Professor Carl Chinn, Cliff Dilloway, Angela Devonport
Richard Drakeford, Mrs Christine Stevens
Robin Norton, Iain Arnold, Colin Brown, Christopher Shores
Peter Somerton, Stratford-upon-Avon, Town Hall
Petr Tomanèák (www.owl.wz.cz)
W/Cdr Paddy Barthropp D.F.C. A.F.C. (who rescued the Rumble Book from certain destruction in 1957)